Here's to more [illegible]
forgiveness and tender-
heartedness in family.
[illegible] G.
Apr '22

Demystifying The Drama Of Marriage

Demystifying The Drama Of Marriage

PENDO K. GALUKANDE
MSc, M.A, LPC (CMFT)

First published in Uganda in 2022

ISBN: 9789970984244

Cover Art & Typesetting: ArmUp Media

Printed in Uganda by:
Honey Badger Ltd
+256 783 097 947
+256 752 298 909

"The definition of a drama is emotional upheaval or turbulence felt in a relationship on an episodic level that has no resolution."

Bonny Albo

Contents

This book is dedicated to those men and women who yearn for more in their marriages; and to my brides Olga, Gloria, Pamela and Irene

Acknowledgements

To the invisible, omnipresent one who has led me on this journey and guides me even now. Thank you for the adventure of life and marriage and bringing so many wonderful people into my life. Life is not possible without you.

I acknowledge Dr. David Jones, my faculty mentor. You came to Regent University just before me and supported me and set me on a good path to develop both as a Christian and as a counsellor. You left as soon as that work was done. Thank you for giving me critical comments on the first drafts of this manuscript.

Thanks to Rachel Barrows who helped me as another subject expert and for the many reflections we have shared.

To Rachel, Sham and Vanessa Lancelloti, my classmates, for committing to write for the world. Sham, for going ahead of us and publishing, always trailblazing and making things look doable.

To all my Regent professors, especially Dr. Smith, Dr. Jones, Dr. Williams, Dr. Savinsky, Dr. Runyan, Dr. Ripley, Dr. Hourihan, Dr. Newmeyer, Dr. Kent and Dr. Towns, for taking an interest in my development as a counsellor, answering my many questions with much grace and getting me to push past my comfort zone to more growth.

Mr. Kuschel, I do not know if this book was my idea or yours. Thanks for the nudge.

To Dr. Worthington, for generously agreeing to write my foreword and for speaking to my audience in Uganda. REACH changed my life!

To Ary, who gave critical input in this manuscript at the early stages, Harriet with whom we digest all concepts psychological and spiritual, and Julia, my sister, with whom I digest life from birth to now. Dr. Rose Nanyonga and Dr. Dominic Bagenda, who have wholeheartedly supported my academic journey and more. Pastor Jones and Auntie Gertrude Bakimi for the spiritual covering and for loving Moses and me.

To our son Talemwa, who, despite our best parental intentions, has to make his own journey through the ups and downs of marriage. Thank you for your great support during my masters, volunteering to take on more than your fair share of cooking duties during my exams and occasionally putting away those open books overflowing on my desk so that there was a semblance of order in my room. You showed me so much kindness. I love you!

To my husband, who charmed the socks off my feet and led me on this wonderful adventure with all its excitement, both good and bad. You are the kindest, gentlest, most generous person I know. Thank you for choosing to go for gold with me. For loving me the best way you know how, supporting my growth and persevering with me through the drama of marriage with full commitment! So excited to be reaping gold with you.

To my Ugandan counseling fraternity, supervisors, consultants, colleagues, friends: Dr. Ruth Senyonyi who planted the first idea of getting counseling training at Regent University many years ago in the parking lot at Lugogo Mall, Mr Rogers Nsereko my Practicum supervisor, Mrs Barbara Kalumba my first internship supervisor, Mrs Sabrina Wantate, all the colleagues at Butabika Mental Hospital and Makerere Full Gospel Church for great access to couples and clients, the best Practicum and Internship sites in the world!

Mrs. Lois Ochieng, Dr. Simon Kizito and Mrs Maureen Kareebi for mentorship and great encouragement. You guys rock!

To my editor Mr. Paul Kisakye, for great patience with me, steady encouragement and expressing enthusiasm for this message.

Foreword

This book takes you on an adventurous journey, the journey through Pendo's unravelling of her conflicts in her marriage to Moses. But as I read it, I realized it could overlap with my own marriage journey, or yours.

Pendo's marital journey is the driving narrative that keeps us involved in the book, but Pendo works in a lot of the learning that made a positive difference in her marriage. She tells about attachment and how it can be disrupted by BIG-T and little-t traumas. She puts her learning into the context of psychosocial development as discovered by Erik Erikson. Her experiences as she was learning about marriage at a marital and family therapy program at Regent University are integrated by sharing the many practical methods developed by therapists who sought to help people improve their marriage. That practical advice is given in several places in lists of easy-to-follow lessons. She is careful to show you whose ideas influenced her marital transformation, and that leaves the door open for you to follow up with more detailed learning if you wish. During her training, Pendo came into contact with Dr. Jennifer Ripley, a Distinguished Professor at Regent University and one of the experts on the Hope-Focused Approach to marriage. Within this programme, my forgiveness work is featured. I am gratified that Pendo found my Forgiveness model pivotal to her marital journey.

My wife, Kirby, and I have been married for fifty-one years. Of course, we've had moments when we have not been blissfully close, but we've persevered. We've applied lessons we've learned in our professional lives—Kirby is a child development specialist who has studied family relationships for fifty years, and I'm a Clinical Psychologist who has done research on relationships for about forty-five years. We've also been committed to our Christian principles, which provide a common vision for marriage, and being involved in our local church has kept us connected with a community of supportive friends and acquaintances.

Troubled couples often say that their relationship problems stem from poor communication. Pendo admits that she held such a belief early in her journey. But research has shown that poor communication usually is not the cause of relationship troubles. It's the effect. The cause is usually that the emotional bond between the partners has been injured and needs mending. Healing can take time and work.

There are many ways to do that hard work of restoring a vibrant emotional bond, but forgiveness is often one of the starting points. Forgiveness is a prime way of repairing the emotional bond. But there are many others. Somehow our personal space seems always to get cluttered and the only way to put it right is to use energy to keep ordering it. This is true of marriage (and even family and friendship relationships) as well.

Sharing important values—such as commitment to a lasting marriage, to religious values, and to maintaining a good relationship with God—is important to keeping partners oriented toward the same relationship targets—that is, keeping them headed straight down the track for a happy and satisfying marriage. But even when romantic partners diverge in their aim, it is essential to continue to have faith that the relationship can be restored to a common track. Partners grow at different rates and in different directions, so getting a bit out of sync at times is almost inevitable. But drawing on religious values, a common view of marriage, and a commitment that both partners will work to put the energy needed into the relationship. Those commitments will keep partners talking when it's hard to talk and keep them working to resolve their differences when the differences seem to be as wide as an ocean.

Everett L. Worthington, Jr.
Forgiveness Expert
Commonwealth Professor Emeritus
Virginia Commonwealth University

Introduction

Not too long ago, I was asked to be the maid of honour to a young lady who seeks wisdom and asks profound questions. It was the night before her wedding and I was performing my maid of honour duties of telling her about the intricacies of the bedroom part of marriage. I did not anticipate that she had something on her mind beyond the topic at hand.

Somewhere along the way, there was a lull in the conversation and she asked, "Pendo, what makes marriage hard?"

For a moment, I could not believe she had asked that question. I had expected all other sorts of questions to do with the first night, but not this one. I momentarily considered telling her that marriage was not hard. You have to be kind to the little ones.

The truth, however, was that I was going through a hard season in my own marriage. The honeymoon had ended with a thud and, at that point, marriage was much harder than I had anticipated.

But what was I to tell her? It was her last night as a single woman. Was I to mar it with sad stories?

In my silence, she added, "I mean, loving someone, how hard can that be?"

"Oh, dear!" I thought. "She is not going to let up, is she? She really does want an answer."

I fumbled around for answers. But I had none. Here I was, married for nearly twenty years, and I was as befuddled as someone who had not been married before.

Indeed, why was my marriage hard? Why couldn't we just get along?

Like her, I had gone into marriage full of hope (what an understatement!) and thought it would be easy. My fiancé and I loved each other more than anyone on earth. We pledged love and commitment to one other. What could go wrong? We were both decent people: reasonably successful socially, morally, academically, and spiritually. We had all the makings of success. However, we too ran into problems that we did not expect and could not solve on our own.

I do not recall my answer to Elaine then, but this book is my attempt at answering her question.

I started writing this book in the middle of my master's training in Marital and Family Counselling in Virginia, USA. The information I was finding during my training was clarifying my understanding of relationships and transforming my marriage and it was just too valuable for me to keep to myself. I had hoped that there were clear concepts about marriage that I could learn to help myself and I was overjoyed to find them.

"I could eat my textbooks," I wrote in one of my circular letters back home. I wanted to bring all my friends to my university but could not. So, the next logical thing was to write down as much as I could to share with other married people, especially those who, like me, had finished the honeymoon stage and come upon the hard part of marriage. Those who could not crack the mystery of marriage.

Like most girls I know, I had grown up to have a set of romantic dreams, of being swept off my feet and living a wild romance. When I met Moses, this was exactly what happened. We had many good honeymoon years. However, after a while, the romance gave way to a pattern of conflict.

"There should be a husband school," I sometimes complained to my girlfriends in frustration. We all *knew* that if only our husbands learnt to love us right, we would be the *perfect* wives.

Meanwhile, in the husband camp: "If only our wives could be happy!" the men lamented, thinking they would be happy if their wives could just be happy.

Now, with my eyes fully opened, I think both camps were wrong. We don't just need a wife school or a husband school. What we need is much more: a marriage school or a relationship school where we are equipped with knowledge and skills to be successful at marriage.

But first, we need to understand the workings of marriage. Why is it so easy to fall in love and yet so hard to stay in love? Why do we fall into a pattern of fighting with our spouses? It used to seem like such a mystery.

In this book, I will share how this marriage pattern of conflict was demystified for me. I can now understand what is going on when Moses and I fight, and I understand the coded language that fighting couples bring into my therapy room too. I think this basic understanding and some training should be compulsory for every human being.

Marriage is one of the greatest determinants of our health and satisfaction in life, yet we spend over eighteen years in school without a single class on how to be successful in marriage! Apart from knowledge, there are skills needed to stop conflicts. I will highlight the ones I found most impactful during my training, skills that I will continue to practice for the rest of my life.

I have not found this knowledge in many of the marriage books commonly available to everyday people, and so I am writing to bridge the gap.

I have a master's degree in Marriage and Family Counselling through a curriculum and teaching methods accredited by the Council for Accreditation of Counselling and Related Educational Programs, the organization that governs counselling education in the US. I have been married for more than twenty-four years and have an adult son. I have worked with other married people, read a tonne of books and scientific papers, watched endless videos, done so many courses, and have been part of a research project on marriage. I have applied the principles I learnt in my master's program to my marriage and I am seeing my marriage transform. I do not want to say this glibly to anyone in a hurting marriage. I know that marriage pain can be the worst pain in the world. I have experienced it. The hope I am offering you is that, first of all, you can understand what is going on in your marriage. Secondly, if you apply the principles that govern relationships that I offer in this book, you can rise out of your conflict, and at worst, whether the marriage works out or not, you will be in a much better place to thrive as an individual. This is because these principles affect your mental health and wellbeing, and affect your whole life, not just your marriage.

1

Marriage in My Ugandan Context

I am a Muganda. Our tribe is the largest and most dominant tribe in Uganda. In my culture, the bride-to-be is prepared for marriage by her aunt, her father's sister, called a senga. Sengas have a list of 101 ground rules on marriage that they verbally pass on to the young bride. A lot of advice is whispered in the privacy of a bedroom about how the young bride should keep her union alive, how to look after herself and how to look after her husband. I skipped this preparation before I got married. My designated senga lived in the village and I lived in the city. She and I only had a very short time together before my wedding. Nonetheless, the other sengas who lived in the city did say things to me in passing that fit the common marital senga advice.

A common phrase that will be said to the young bride is, "Obufumbo buzibu!" meaning, "Marriage is hard!" Most of the preparation in my context seemed to centre around this theme:

Marriage is hard! The long list of marital dos and don'ts also suggests that marriage is hard.

One of the hardest parts about marriage is the conflict between husband and wife! There are other issues surrounding marriage but this seems to be the greatest of them all. The sengas do not explicitly tell you what will be hard about marriage. They will typically spend more time on the actions the bride should take to prevent marital conflict or manage the situation if marital conflicts arise.

To me, all the advice felt like warnings. I started to feel fear rise up within me. Why did it feel like I was being sent out to war instead of love? Why was everyone seemingly so afraid for me? It was a mystery, but I was so in love and I was going to have a ball! We were headed to cloud nine. Only Moses and I knew it. I chose to ignore the mindset that was being pushed on me.

As a young bride, if you happen to return to these aunties to report that your marriage is hard, the typical answer is, "Munange guma!" Roughly translated, this means, "My dear, persevere." Whereas it is comforting to know that marital conflict is a common human experience, it does little to actually help the young bride. The sengas do not have answers for why marriages fall into patterns of conflict. Men and women alike will talk about the different conflicts that come up in marriage today. I did not find any satisfactory answer to the question, "Why do couples tend to conflict?" Besides developing rules for marriage, it is often a mystery why marriages are prone to problems in the first place.

As we think about marital conflict, a discussion on divorce is warranted. How successful is the marriage institution? Unfortunately, we do not have the data in Uganda to tell for sure; and even in the US where data is more readily available, we still cannot tell for sure. Divorce rates are hard to ascertain because it is not easy to agree on how the measurement is done. I could not find research that solidly backs the commonly thrown around idea that 50% of the marriages in the US end in divorce.

This is what I was able to find. In the US the CDC's National Center for Health Statistics (NCHS) publishes the number of marriages and the number of divorces annually. The data on the official NCHS website collected between the years 2000-2019 indicate the marriage count in the US as two million marriages a year and about 800,000 divorces a year. A closer look at the data shows that divorce rates dropped from 944,000 in the year 2000 to 746,000 in 2019; marriage rates also dropped from 2.3 million to 2 million annually for the same time period. Whereas the trend shows a decline in divorce rates, it also shows a decline in marriage rates. It is important to note that this data excludes certain states like California which account for 40 million people out of 300 million Americans – a whopping 13%. The data is not helpful in telling us the success rate of marriages in the US, and it certainly is not saying that divorce rates are 50%. What we all want to know, and what would be really helpful is "of 100 marriages that begin, how many are typically likely to survive and be happy marriages?"

In Uganda, we often pride ourselves in lower rates of divorce than the western world. In the only research I could find, completed between 1988-2011, the Ugandan divorce rate was put at about 30-40% (Clark & Brauner-Otto, 2015). The research is outdated and there is a need for follow-up studies. Also, it is well known in Uganda that societal pressure to keep up appearances in marriage is high. As one preacher put it, "In Uganda, many couples live separate lives under the same roof." So, it appears as if marriage is more successful in Uganda, but is it really? It is not enough to judge the success rates of marriage by divorce rates alone. My hypothesis from interviewing many married people is that the real rates of success (happy marriages) are much lower than the statistics will tell us if we only go by divorce rates.

I had gone into marriage not believing the sengas. If they had difficult marriages, that did not mean that mine was going to be difficult.

However, I had come upon a cycle of conflict in my marriage. The sengas were right after all – Marriage is hard! Moses and I were fighting constantly and seemed unable to stop! During this time, I found that I could not fully grasp what was going on. We sought counselling a few times, yet we remained with many unanswered questions. There seemed to be no satisfactory working theory that would help us grasp what the real root of the problem was then. What chances did we have of finding real solutions? It was all a mystery!

So yes, I want to agree that marriage is hard due to couple conflict, but I have learnt some things about marriage that make it far easier to understand, and I am so excited and want to shout my findings from the rooftops! I now understand why Moses and I were in conflict. In addition, I can tell you how much easier it has become because not only do we understand the underlying story of our conflict, but we also found workable solutions. Our marriage is going through a transformation! I say "going through" because the work is a lifelong process. Nonetheless, I am more satisfied with my marriage now than I was in the past, and I am no longer terrified of it ending!

The hard things couples bring into the counselling room

Many hard things bring married couples to counselling. The most commonly stated reason the world over that couples give is communication problems. However, when you scratch beneath that surface, often you find deeper problems like unfaithfulness, addictions (both behavioural and substance), financial difficulties, domestic violence, conflicts over religion and these days even politics, lack of respect, lack of support, lack of love, failure of companionship, differences in parenting, unequal power, infrequent sex, and more. The list could go on. During my training, I discovered that what a couple state is the issue, is rarely the real issue. These troubles are mostly the surface presentation of something deeper and simpler.

Communication failures are rarely about listening and speaking. Erroneously diagnosing poor communication as the most common marriage failure has led to communication being one of the main topics at marriage seminars. I do not know how many conferences I have attended that taught skills such as reflective listening, where you repeat what the other person is saying. Many of these communication solutions are so superficial and, in our case, yielded poor results.

The solutions that I read about in marriage books and received in therapy were just too superficial. For me, marriage tools such as the five love languages, spiritual foundations, and others, simply did not transform my marriage. The concepts in these books are brilliant but they could not stop our pattern of conflict! There just had to be more!

To say that I was frustrated is an understatement. I combed through mountains of books. We went for marital and individual counselling and did not find solutions. It is very disconcerting to have a problem and not be clear on what the root of the problem is. It is like fighting an invisible enemy. What are the chances of winning?

I am a big picture person. I need to understand the big picture in order to make sense of the small details of everyday life. I like solving problems and I find that good, sustainable solutions require me to broadly understand a system before attempting to fix it. However, I found most approaches to marital problems did not give me a comprehensive and logical understanding of the marital conflict dilemma. As humans, we have a need to understand. We have a need to make sense of things. When we can understand our problems and make sense of them, our troubles feel less burdensome, and it becomes much easier to go about finding solutions.

What I hope to do with this book is to help you gain a deeper understanding of marital conflict, so you too can find your solutions. Additionally, I also point out tools that have worked for me in my marriage that are within your reach.

Before I delve into why couples conflict, I want to share some immediate relief that is offered by viewing the marital conflict as part of a bigger picture. The main reason for this is to help one realize and understand that extreme marital conflict is a common stage of most marriages. That is all that it is, a stage. And there are other stages. It is so common and therefore considered the norm. What the sengas were trying to say is simply this: expect it, don't be thrown off by it! It tends to come to most people that get into marriage. Secondly, this knowledge helps you to understand it will pass and give way to other stages of marriage. If you can hold on, it is bound to pass. In this book, I will teach you how to accelerate your growth through this phase.

The idea of stages of marriage was beautifully introduced to me a few years ago in Ndoa. Ndoa is a popular marriage course in the East African region by Muriithi and Carol Wanjau and it is offered by the Mavuno churches. In Ndoa, we were taught about the four stages in the life cycle of marriage as

1. Dream,
2. Drama,
3. Discovery and
4. Depth.

This categorization is immediately helpful in gauging which stage of marriage you are in right now. According to the Wanjaus, the Dream stage is early in the honeymoon years, where spouses see each other in an overly positive light and even downplay their weaknesses. During this time, you think your match was made in heaven. This stage is characterized by intense positive feelings, where the passion and admiration for each other are through the roof! At this stage, your partner can do no wrong, I mean even when they do, it really is insignificant compared to their dazzling good qualities!

The next stage is called Drama. This is the stage I try to demystify in this book. Drama is all about marital conflict! During Drama, your spouse's failures gradually become glaring, they are almost all you can see, and it is not uncommon for married people in this stage to think they made a mistake in choosing their spouse. They may wonder how blind they were at an earlier stage to miss seeing their partner's flaws. As a therapist, I think some couples enter drama early before they are married and come to the wedding day in the throes of conflict, the Dream stage having already faded. During drama, many couples consider divorce. The pain is too intense and at some point, the couple gives up hope of resolving their conflict and agree to part ways and at least be out of their pain.

Several couples make it through Drama to a more peaceful stage called Discovery where the couple gives up unrealistic dreams and accepts their reality. The couple may see themselves much more as business partners than as lovers. "Some marriages survive divorce in Drama stage only to 'amicably divorce' at this stage because the marriage just got boring," the Wanjaus write in Ndoa. Often, the grass seems greener on the other side. This too is a normal stage of development. If you are in this stage, this too will pass.

According to the Wanjaus, only a few marriages make it to the fourth and final stage: Depth. This is where the couple is deeply vulnerable to each other, celebrate their differences and work as a team. It is my understanding (not that the Wanjaus said this) that the differentiating factor that sets the few couples that get to Depth from the ones that stay in Discovery is that the Depth couples learn certain skills that they did not possess earlier. They learn how to build authentic intimacy.

Although this book is about getting out of Drama stage, I will introduce the tools that I am convinced lead a couple to the Depth stage. First, let me tell you our Dream and Drama stories. Meeting Moses was a Dream. It was and still is one of the most outstanding highlights of my life.

2

The Dream

I am the last born of three children. I was born in the 1970s, in the days of President Idi Amin, the days of political turmoil and military brutality in Uganda. The days when heads of families were picked up by unidentified people never to be seen again. My Taata (father), Pio Zirimu, was a professor of linguistics at Makerere University. My Maama (mother), Elvania Zirimu, was an English teacher, playwright and dance choreographer. When I was born, my family lived in the Makerere University staff housing. We were part of a very diverse university community.

Taata had a mild temperament and was easy-going, while Maama was the disciplinarian and had a bit of a temper when crossed. Apparently, she was much fiercer before my day and had mellowed a bit by the time I came along.

I was a very sensitive child. I needed more affection than the average human, or at least more than my brother and sister, Lwanga and Julia, four years and nine years older than me respectively. Lwanga has a lively mind full of humour. He liked to pull pranks and the two of us often got into fights. Julia, our eldest, is serene and kind. Being the first born, she carries a sense of responsibility for the two of us to this day. When we were young, she was always very protective of me and tried to keep the peace between my brother and me.

My family liked to jest and tease a lot. Being a sensitive child, my feelings were easily hurt and I used to cry several times a day. My family developed code language around my crying. They used to talk about the likelihood of 'rain', a code word for tears. If someone said, "It looks like it might rain," they really meant, I was on the verge of tears again. At some point, I figured out what they were referring to and felt betrayed that they were speaking about me amongst themselves.

My family, like any other family, had its ups and downs, but was overall stable and loving for us as children, until tragedy struck one day.

It was 1977, and our family was in Lagos, Nigeria, for an extended visit on account of my father who was leading up a major event, the Africa Festival of Arts (known as FESTAC). There was a lot of uneasiness for the family around his appointment to this position. There were people who felt that they were more deserving of the role. There was palpable tension around his being head of FESTAC. In that leadership role, Taata had to make many critical decisions, including which lectures, plays and performances were going to be allowed onto the programme and which ones were not, which voices were to be heard and which ones were not. The other layer to this tremulous responsibility was that much of the content of the performances was sensitive since the issue of our Africanness and blackness in many countries was and still is a delicate issue.

My family heard rumours that my father was a marked man. He was cautioned not to drink the office tea, nor eat anything that was served to him alone. One day during our stay in Nigeria, he was taken ill and admitted to hospital. Maama, who had taken him to the hospital, was instructed by the medical personnel to leave him at the hospital for the night. The next day, Maama arrived at the hospital and found him dead. The first post-mortem was not very helpful in pointing out a cause of death. However, a second post-mortem, from the University Hospital in Lagos stated the cause of death as poisoning. We had left Uganda as an intact family of five. Only four of us returned alive to Uganda. We returned with Taata's body. My siblings and I were fatherless, and my Maama husbandless. My mother and siblings were devastated. However, I did not really understand what had happened. I am told I played in the sand by Taata's grave during the burial.

Three years later, we were just getting accustomed to life without Taata when Maama was appointed ambassador of Uganda to Ghana. She married one of her close friends Cliff, and in preparation for the move to Ghana we had packed up all our belongings. She and Cliff went out to attend a farewell party in their honour. On their way back home, they had a terrible car accident around Kyambogo. They were rushed to Mulago hospital where Cliff survived.

But Maama, my closest friend in the family, died.

I was six years old.

This was when my super emotional self completely shut down. Whereas I used to cry at the drop of a hat, this time, there were no tears. I was too heartbroken for that. I sat in the corner of our home at the dining table, which had been pushed to the side while Maama's body, sagging heavily in an old green bed cover, was brought into the house. I was beyond grief. I was frozen.

I watched the proceedings and overheard some people comment that they were surprised I was not even crying. They could see that something was not right about my reaction, but they did not understand the depth of my grief. In fact, from their comments, they thought I was not so affected.

Not long afterwards, my siblings and I were adopted by family relations with whom we were close socially. We used to visit them in the good days when our parents were alive. They had a grand house and we had wonderful playtimes when we visited. I looked forward to the day they would pick us up, especially since our home had become frighteningly quiet and solemn without Maama and the days also seemed to have become darker. The shade from the trees in the garden seemed to block out all the sun and it was as if the sun was reluctant to come out each day after Maama's death.

My new parents had four children of their own and several other relatives in the home and were extremely generous towards all of us. We lacked for nothing materially. We still had wonderful times of play, and the games were all the more fun because we were so many in the house. We were at least thirteen children in the house on most days.

Whereas my new family did their best to care for us, I remained with a great longing for Maama. No one really understood my heartbreak. In their kindness, my new parents thought it was best to not talk about my parents in order not to hurt my feelings or bring back the sad memory of Maama's death. Once in a while, my sister and a couple of family friends talked to me about Maama. Other than that, there was a great silence around my parents' life and death. There was a vacuum where parental voices and images should have been stored in my mind. There were signs that all was not well internally. I was less receptive to people, a bit withdrawn at home, but it was not clear to anyone that my heartbreak was significant and might need professional attention.

In time, I was old enough to go to university and although I had many male friends, I had decided that I was not going to actively look for a dating relationship. I wanted to be active in serving God and did not want any distractions. I was friendly but would get rather serious around boys especially if they showed signs of being romantically interested in me.

As university life progressed, I met Moses. I liked him the moment I met him. He was the head of all the fellowships at the university and was on his pastoral duties to my hall of residence, Africa, a ladies-only hall, when we first met. He carried his tall, lanky, handsome self quietly and respectably. He dressed like half student, half lecturer (or professor as they call them in the US). He wore a navy-blue blazer with gold buttons, long-sleeved shirt and Mickey Mouse socks!

Moses was introduced by the leader of our hall fellowship as the chairman of all the fellowships at the university. He was a fourth-year medical student. The leader of our hall fellowship, a girl I admired and looked up to, introduced him with a touch of awe. I was intrigued.

The fellowship started off with singing and prayer and at Bible study time, we broke into smaller groups. I was delighted when Moses ended up in my little group. He presented his ideas with such grace and wisdom that I felt I really wanted to get to know him.

It took about two more years before we started to interact more closely. I was usually exhilarated when I left him. There was something mysterious about him. Whereas I was mostly an open book, easily sharing my life story with new friends, Moses was more reserved and did not initially reveal too much of his life story. He left a lot of himself hidden and I had to probe to find out more. I found this trait extremely attractive. I was often surprised at what interesting things I discovered about him through my probing. I was enchanted!

He, on the other hand, was also besotted with me.

Apart from his intriguing mind, and his quiet ways, I found Moses as a gentle, reliable person that was extremely kind. For example, once we were at a huge youth retreat of several universities at lunchtime. I did not have a plate, and with all the people milling about, I had no idea where to get a plate. I made my way to him as our leader, and after my enquiry, he started to point me in the direction of the plates where I saw a long queue. Suddenly, he dropped his pointing hand, turned to me and handed me his plate with a smile. His kindness caught me off guard. I was touched, but I tried not to show it. I gratefully took the plate and went away.

At another gathering that our hall of residence was hosting, I was up and down serving guests with no time to enjoy the goings-on. Moses was in the crowd. On one of my trips to the kitchen as I walked past him, he touched my arm, I stopped and turned, expecting to be asked for service, yet when I looked at him, he was holding out his plate with a biscuit. At first, I was perplexed. I looked at it and then his kind face and understanding dawned on me. I had not eaten all afternoon since I was busy as one of the hosts. I was hungry and here he was, offering me his biscuit.

What a sweet gesture! Beyond the biscuit, the seriousness I had reserved for friendly boys was being melted by his kindness and thoughtfulness!

If I told you the whole story, this book would be twice its length! Suffice it to say, there were several interactions like these. I was starting to really like this guy.

The short version of our story is that I fell madly in love with Moses and was delighted to discover that he too was in love with me. During our courtship, whereas we both seemed to want to be around each other equally, Moses as a medical student with a part-time job was busier than me. We spent as much time as we could together, but I felt it was nearly never enough. We wrote letters in-between (this was the age just before mobile phones) and visited each other.

We had a three-year courtship and were married in 1997, shortly after I graduated from the university.

Like me, Moses had endured a lot of loss in his family. During his university days, he had lost his father, a sister, and nearly lost a brother in a bomb blast at the taxi park in Kampala. This had all taken place in five short years. Add the rigour of medical school which in itself is brutal, and you can imagine the emotional depletion he carried. So, we both looked forward to starting our own family and being a comfort to each other. We were giddy with excitement as our wedding day approached. We could not believe that our dream was coming true.

He was my first boyfriend and as a much-sheltered church girl, I did not suspect that the honeymoon years would ever end. I had not read romance novels growing up and I had largely kept away from adult movies. I usually hung out with girls who talked about God and did not talk much about romance and relationships. I honestly thought I was the luckiest girl in the world and, unlike all the other miserable women who ended up marrying the wrong men and were now unhappy, I was the only fortunate one who had found my soulmate, or so I thought. My heart could burst with happiness. I now understand the sympathetic gazes and knowing nods the older women used to give me when they came upon the high hopes and dreams I held for my marriage.

3

The Drama Begins

Our first years in marriage were as I had imagined they would be. I was on cloud nine! I felt that I completely belonged, safe in Moses's love. Moses said I pampered him and he felt really special in the way I treated him. We started out living in very supportive communities. Moses was a doctor in a rural Christian community and we lived happily and simply, surrounded by people that were supportive of our relationship. Even when we returned to the city for Moses to pursue further studies, we lived in Doctor's village in Mulago, a community made up of doctors' families, where we were able to organize our lives in a way that gave us both much satisfaction. I was, therefore, completely unprepared for the hard times in marriage. A shift happened and it happened so subtly. It crept up on us without our noticing. It is a wonder how two seemingly well-adjusted human beings are happy and full of hope before marriage; they get on with their lives, have meaningful connections with friends and family, are doing well in their careers, and have a loving relationship with God. Then they meet this wonderful partner that they have appraised as good for them, get married, hoping that their happiness will increase, but instead find that they are now more unhappy than when they started.

To put this in perspective, let me tell you a bit about what life was like before marriage. At the university, before Moses and I met, we enjoyed close relationships with a variety of friends and kept in touch with key family members. I really enjoyed campus life. Having spent six years of secondary school in an extremely regimented Roman Catholic convent school, I was not accustomed to the freedom afforded by university life. It was exhilarating! For the first time in my life, I had unlimited time with friends and was allowed to do whatever activity I wanted when I wanted. If I slept in, even on a weekday morning, no one reprimanded me. I generally attended all my lectures. My out of class schedule was a little hectic. I was part of a choir, attended about three to four fellowships a week, not to mention nearly daily prayer sessions. During my years at the university, I wrote a play and directed it, organized outings with my friends and started two businesses. In short, I was thriving.

Moses was a medical student, yet he managed to oversee the whole Christian Union made up of several hall and faculty fellowships, a money-generating project for the fellowship, and he had a business and a job on the side as well. I was mostly happy at university and it appears that Moses was too.

Judging from these parameters, it does not make sense that we would not be more successful at happiness in marriage together than we were alone. In marriage, we were each making adjustments but it seems these adjustments were not what the other expected.

I had been fiercely independent before I was married, but I became quite dependent on Moses after we were married. I wanted him to either sanction my leisure activities or join me in them. He, on the other hand, was expecting me to carry on as the independent person he had met. He wanted me to figure out what I wanted out of a given week and go about getting it with or without him. With hindsight, I can see that when I got married, I retired from the job of making myself happy. I considered it Moses's job now, and like a terrible employer, I had not only not informed him of his new responsibilities, I also had not given him training. Meanwhile, I was fuming that he was failing badly at the task of making me happy!

I wanted him to be a lot more available to me than he expected to be. Disappointment started to set in. On the surface, our troubles started out as fighting about the amount of time we spent with each other and how that time should be spent. I liked for us to be together alone for long times. I valued closeness. Moses, on the other hand, enjoyed working hard and long. He valued his work and independence. We had little appreciation for each other's values. Moses did not understand how I could want to spend so much time with him and I could not understand why he would want to work so long and hard. We also approached companionship very differently. I needed time, but he was not around most of the time. I valued more interaction; he valued more space. When he was home, he was content to just be watching TV in the same space with me, but for me, watching TV did not count at all as companionship. It was zero points gained as time together. I wanted to have intense talks about life, to know each other's internal worlds, to look into each other's eyes and declare our love forever. I was the hopeless romantic and believed I could spend endless hours with my husband in these heart-to-heart talks.

There was another major difference between us. I had a very deep-seated belief that time was running out and anything I needed to do, I needed to do quickly. Moses, on the other hand, seemed to feel that we had a long marriage and life ahead of us and would get to things in time. I needed us to spend as much time together daily and he felt we could spend time together weekly.

I needed decisions made quickly, while he felt decisions could be made sometime in the future. In short, I have a certain impatience about life and he seemed eternally patient with life.

There was always this push and pull between us. With time, we started to construe each other's actions as personal affronts and eventually we were having strong disagreements. I started to think that Moses really just did not like me a lot. In my mind, if he did, he would want to spend as much time with me as I wanted to spend with him. I felt like the prized wife that he had won and now abandoned to the home. It felt as if, having finished the task of winning my love, he was now pursuing his career and was totally absorbed by it. I felt discarded. I was so envious of his career. His career felt like 'the other woman' to me.

These negative thoughts led me to feel very lonely in my marriage. The lonelier I felt, the more disappointed I became. My disappointment grew into anger that spilt out of me in the form of criticism. I felt more and more unloved by him, and he felt more and more despised by me. The more unloved I felt the more critical of him I became.

Moses had believed the most loving thing he could do for me was not to spend the day looking at me but to go about his work with all the vigour he could muster so that he could support me and the family we were planning to have in such a way that we would lack nothing for the rest of our lives. He was carrying a great burden, compounded by the fact that we also had a relatively big financial responsibility towards the extended family. He felt overwhelmed by this responsibility, but never complained about it.

I was unaware of how burdened he was. I felt that his work was the enemy and I attacked it. For him, this was the worst thing I could do. The very thing he was giving me as a sacrifice of his love was the thing for which I criticized him. I wanted him to be like those husbands that come home at 5 pm to attend to their families and are thriving at work and at home. I had a high standard for him, especially on the home front, and he had an especially high standard for himself at work and expected me to cut him some slack at home. Our fights started around these matters and spread into other parts of our lives.

Moses was better at meeting his own companionship needs but also had some unmet expectations that he was not good at voicing. That was just not the way he was put together. I would only discover his needs when I probed. This reticence that attracted me to him, was now a source of frustration for me.

Moses figured that if he did not put a strain on the relationship by making more demands, perhaps I would be happier. Also, if he worked harder to provide, maybe I would be pleased with him. What frustrated him was the way I constantly criticized him for not meeting my companionship and emotional needs. He felt that I was unfairly critical and negative because he was contributing in other ways. Eventually, he who had been the object of my passionate admiration started to feel that he was not good enough for me and that nothing he could do would satisfy me. He felt helpless. He too was getting desperate albeit quietly.

It is really painful to fight so consistently with the person you are most intimate with in life. Our relationship was deteriorating slowly. It got crazier and crazier until I felt that if something did not change, the marriage was not going to survive this Drama.

In the midst of these fights, we were still attracted to each other and I cannot say that the marriage was devoid of affection. So, it boggled our minds that we just could not stop fighting. Here we were, married to the person of our dreams, and more miserable than we had been without each other. With time, though, the conflict was swallowing up all the affection we felt towards each other. What was wrong with us? What happened? Who took away all the power for us to make ourselves happy? Who took away the potential to dream and the eagerness to live life? Later, I demonstrate that this dynamic is about a system that operates in all romantic relationships. It is not as complicated as it seemed then!

Although it took long for me to admit it to myself, I was in distress and I was unable to understand, name or own the process. I thought I was in distress because I was not getting the love I needed. We had been fighting for years and I did not know how to take away the pain. What I usually did in those moments of pain was to reach for something that would numb my pain, but most of these things did not effectively comfort me. I often reached for activities like reading novels, mindlessly browsing social media, writing in my journal, and complaining to friends. These were all helpful for a time, but not enough. These strategies would temporarily give me a sense of control but then the effect would wear off and I would feel guilty sometimes for having wasted so much time.

The truth was, what Moses and I were fighting for was not time. We just could not resolve the time issue because there was a much deeper issue at play. Most of my distress was about feeling disconnected and the solutions I used were not always helpful in making me feel connected.

4

Emotional Bonds

Many couples come to counselling in the Drama stage of marriage. The particular issues in the drama initially seem to be as varied as the number of couples that show up in the counselling room. Both professional and lay counsellors go about trying to solve various problems that bring couples to the counselling room. The themes might be differences in parenting, infrequent sex, finances, you name it. In the past, all we could do as therapists was to focus on the issue and try to give couples tools to solve the presenting problem. Yet, at the end of the day, there is one problem that is foundational and sets the tone for the whole marriage; one problem that is often missed that sets the stage for the greatest difficulty in marriage. This one problem, if solved, makes marriage much easier and enables couples to solve their own problems. The problem is the lack of a secure emotional bond or an emotional attachment.

According to experts in marriage, Dr. Ripley and Dr. Ev Worthington, couples who are unable to form secure emotional bonds struggle the most in marriage. "Those who are able to form secure emotional bonds (otherwise called secure attachment in psychology) are able to meet their needs both independently and interdependently and tend to thrive." A lot of research shows that this in fact is the most critical factor in marriage. Yet in marital preparation, this is a factor that is hardly talked about. I suspect that even after reading this idea, the significance of it is likely to be missed by most people. So, allow me to build this point a little bit. Think about the parental bond. Most parents have such a strong bond with their children that no matter what the children do, the relationship in the majority of cases endures all manner of adverse circumstances. Our getting on with people is less about their skills and behaviour and more about our bonds with them.

You may wonder, if the answer is so simple, why don't we all just get about forming secure emotional bonds with each other? Well, it is not that easy. Emotional bonds are not made by snapping our fingers. You cannot forge an emotional bond by faking it. There were times when Moses and I would be fighting and I would reach out to hold hands, but the stiffness in the handholding sent me back a message that we could be at opposite ends of the earth with all our handholding.

Before we can begin to form emotional bonds, each one of us has an existent way of being that makes it easier or harder to form these emotional bonds. Our ability to form strong emotional bonds or secure attachments with others was determined by the way we were raised and a plethora of other influencing factors like genetic factors and even one's mental health as I will share. Attachment happens in our brains. Our brains are like computers and are programmed to attach. Some people securely attach, that is, form strong emotional bonds easily. But the majority of us will struggle, to varying degrees, in forming secure attachments. The good news is, the work can be done. Moses and I are doing the work and we see a remarkable change in our marriage. I will share our transformation story primarily from my point of view and the steps I took in the chapters that follow. But first, let me explain the science of forming secure bonds, the science of attachment.

The idea of attachment was first developed by a man named John Bowlby in 1957. He had grown up in a British aristocratic family and had been very close to his governess. Bowlby was heartbroken when he was separated from his governess and this experience was a strong influence on his understanding of relationships and what governs them. Human beings experience heartache or distress when attachment bonds are broken or strained. It is not hard to understand attachment. Every child is born with an innate desire to attach, that is, to form an emotional bond with a caring adult. Attachment ensures that our needs for safety, comfort and pleasure are met. Although attachment is an invisible quality, there is evidence of it that even a layperson can observe. The four observable characteristics of attachment that were first observed in young children are:

1. safe haven,

2. secure base,

3. proximity and

4. separation distress.

Safe haven: The baby will suckle, cuddle, play with and smile at their carer and seem most at ease around them. This is because the attachment figure of the child is the provider of emotional and physical nurturance, the source of comfort and pleasure, but also the protector from danger. The person to return to when threatened. This is how the characteristic of a safe haven plays out in real life.

Secure base: When the child starts to get mobile, they will usually become curious about the world beyond their carer but usually keep returning to the carer for interpretation, sometimes pointing to ask the carer to name objects. For the baby to explore the world, they need to have a "headquarters", a reference point from which the rest of the world is understood and interpreted. The carer is a reliable and trusted source to help interpret and explore the world.

Proximity: Another aspect that characterizes attachment is the distance or closeness babies will seek to maintain with the attachment figure. Even when the baby goes exploring, they will want the attachment figure to not be too far away. Children seem to feel safer when the carer is within sight. At a younger age, the distance is much shorter. I observed this with my son; initially, he would mostly play if I was somewhere within the house, generally a 5-10 metres distance. Eventually at about the age of four, he would go outside and play with his friends but always return within an hour or less as if to check that I was still there for him. As he grew older the distance grew and the check-ins became less frequent. Now he lives in another country and I am confident that he still feels safe and supported.

Separation distress: This is another easy to observe aspect of attachment. Babies are unhappy when they are separated from their attachment figure. They usually become distressed and cry.

You may wonder what all of this has to do with marriage. I will make the connection, just bear with me for a while as we get in some more understanding afforded to us by observing babies.

The design of a little human being facilitates attachment. As a zoologist, I was taught that the delicate smell of young offspring, the big eyes, the small size and soft skin, are all important in eliciting sympathetic care from others. Even a little tiger looks like something you should protect when you see it. If you put your finger near a new-born, they will naturally cling onto that finger. When babies hold our little finger or request to be held, there is a parallel process usually going on psychologically. These little human beings are also reaching out to us emotionally. They are open to care and pull on our heartstrings by design. Science shows that children will attempt to form a secure emotional bond with their primary caregiver. This is perhaps the greatest determinant of their survival in life because once a bond is established, the caregiver will do a lot to protect the vulnerable offspring. Therefore, an emotional bond means life. The absence of an emotional bond means death.

Now, let's get a little deeper into attachment. There are primarily two types of attachment: secure attachment and insecure attachment. These technical terms are not hard to understand. The basic meaning is the same as in plain English, although there is a lot more to the terms in science. We will get to that. For now, it is enough to know that a secure attachment is good and an insecure attachment is not good.

Whereas there is only one type of secure attachment, there are three different types of insecure attachment in children.

1. Avoidant

2. Anxious and

3. Disorganized attachment

Interestingly, some of the first research in understanding these types of attachment was done in Uganda in the 1950s by Mary Ainsworth, a development psychologist. She carried out an experiment in which infants less than eighteen months old were separated and reunited with their mothers. She found that all of the children reacted in only three recognized ways upon reunification with their mothers. All the children were distressed when they noticed that their mothers were no longer with them in the room. However, on being reunited, there were distinct differences in how the infants received their mothers. Some immediately went to the mother, accepted her soothing and later went back to play (secure). Some went to the mother for comfort but took some time to be soothed and remained upset and clingy afterwards, unwilling to go back to play (anxious). Finally, others seemed to avoid the mother even when reunited, either refusing to meet her gaze or turning their backs on the mother (avoidant). These three styles were named secure, anxious and avoidant attachment styles respectively.

Later research by other scientists revealed another style of attachment in which the child gave mixed signals: going towards the mother, but then flopping down as if giving up, or wanting to be held and then pulling away. This was called disorganized attachment.

Characterization of these attachment styles revealed that secure children have an internal sense that they are worthwhile and believe that people will be trusted and their needs will be met; because of this, they are not fretful. They feel safe in the world and have a default outlook that everything will be okay. On the other hand, insecure children may have any of the following flawed beliefs: "I am not lovable", "I am not worthwhile", "People cannot be trusted" and so on. This makes these children more fretful. Their default outlook to the world is "my needs will not be met."

Avoidantly attached children's primary way of coping with the feelings of insecurity is to pull away and create distance between themselves and their caregivers. On the opposite end of the scale, anxiously attached children cope with feelings of insecurity by being clingy and not wanting to be left alone. They react strongly if they cannot be close. They may want to be held and need a lot more assurance than other children.

The third type of insecure attachment which was discovered in later research, disorganized attachment, may look like a mix of both anxious and avoidant attachment, but it really is about the child not having any strategy of coping with feelings of insecurity.

In it, children alternate between being clingy and creating distance, exhibiting both protestations of distance and aloofness to their caregiver.

Studies indicate that a parent that is attentive to a child, not only physically but also emotionally, and meets the needs of the child in a consistent manner, will help the child to feel secure. On the other hand, families where parents or caregivers are, for whatever reason, not able to meet the needs of a child consistently, or meet the physical needs but not the emotional needs, will tend to yield insecurely attached children.

Some studies show that securely attached children come out of homes where parents meet the children's needs consistently. Anxiously attached children have at least one parent that they were connected to emotionally but their emotional needs were not met consistently or they could also have had a detached parent. Avoidantly attached children could have had physically attentive but emotionally distant parents, while the disorganized attached children usually come from chaotic homes characterized by physical, emotional or substance abuse.

Studies also show that temporary or permanent separation from parents for prolonged periods plus the insufficient emotional nurturing of the child by stand-in carers has an impact on the attachment style of children. One study called "The Forty Thieves" compared a group of emotionally disturbed children who had gotten into trouble for shoplifting with other emotionally disturbed children who were not involved in shoplifting. The shoplifting group had a higher incidence of children having been separated from their mothers for considerable amounts of time. Further research shows that what really makes the difference is how emotionally attuned stand-in carers are to the children after they are separated from their mothers. Obviously, a mother's love is hard to replicate. Differences in relationships with the primary caregiver create a unique psychological map for future relationships and behaviour inside each child. This map is a huge determinant of relationship success that we need to become aware of. The pattern of how we related to our parents in childhood has a huge impact on how we will relate to others in adulthood.

Before we shoot the parents, let us note that the behaviour of parents was impacted by the way they were cared for by their parents, and their parents the same ad-infinitum. We cannot really blame our parents because we cannot prove that parenting is the sole determinant of attachment styles. It appears that personality, genetic makeup and other external circumstances also affect a child's ability to form secure attachment bonds.

In *The Body Keeps the Score,* Bessel van der Kolk wrote, "Children are programmed to choose one particular adult (at most a few) with whom their natural communication system develops. This creates a primary attachment bond. The more responsive the adult is to the child, the deeper the attachment and the more likely the child will develop healthy ways of responding to the people around him .... Having a safe haven promotes self-reliance and instils a sense of sympathy and helpfulness to others in distress. Children get in sync and develop self-awareness, empathy, impulse control and self-motivation."

I dwell on this behaviour in children in a book about marriage because it has a bearing on the marriage relationship. Scientists have found that people tend to keep their childhood attachment style well into adulthood unless something happens to change it.

In adulthood, the four attachment styles are named a little differently:

Four Adult Attachment Styles

Childhood attachment	Adult attachment style
Avoidant attachment	Dismissive avoidant attachment (DA)
Anxious attachment	Anxious preoccupied attachment (AP)
Disorganized attachment	Fearful Avoidant attachment (FA)
Secure attachment	Secure attachment (SA)

The Four adulthood attachment styles are:

Dismissive Avoidant: These people are characterized as being afraid of intimacy. According to Thais Gibson, a professional counsellor and personal development expert, "Avoidants will tend to diminish or repress their emotions, struggle to believe that their emotional needs will be met, will protect their personal space and autonomy, they are easily hurt by criticism and will withdraw to self soothe and need more time to warm back up."

Anxious Preoccupied: These people view love in an obsessive way, with a strong need for constant reciprocation and validation, along with emotional highs and lows, and feelings of jealousy and strong sexual attraction. Anxious Ambivalent (*Ambivalent is another term used to describe this style*) partners tend to be very sensitive to rejection and distance in a romantic relationship. They can move into commitment very quickly and fear abandonment.

Fearful Avoidant: These desire intimacy but also are afraid of being let down. As a result, they may appear both hot and cold, giving off mixed signals. Unlike the other attachment styles, they do not have a particular strategy. In some instances, they are like the Avoidants, creating distance and pushing others away, and in other cases, they may be clingy. They may experience a lot of guilt, are suspicious and fear betrayal. They are passionate and are mostly volatile in relationships. In my view, these are the ones most likely to become verbally and physically abusive partners.

Secure: These folks have a positive view of themselves and others, feel safe in the world, believe that problems are solvable, feel free to express themselves, have a strong ability to regulate their emotions, have empathy towards others, protect their boundaries, and have a strong self-identity. They describe their romantic relationships as friendly, trusting, and happy. They accept their partners regardless of faults. They tend to have long and fulfilling relationships.

An additional layer to attachment is how people in the different groups view themselves and others. Securely attached people tend to have a positive view of themselves and others, anxiously attached people will have a negative view of themselves and a positive view of others, avoidant people will have a positive view of themselves and a negative view of others and fearful avoidants will have a negative view of themselves and a negative view of others.

Summary of Internal Perceptions of Self and Others

	View of self	View of others
Secure	+	+
Anxious	-	+
Avoidant	+	-
Fearful	-	-

In a marriage relationship, especially in marital conflict and drama, attachment dynamics are the invisible forces at play. The real mystery lies in the attachment psychology of the marriage partners.

I had read a number of books and seen a few therapists in Uganda, but none of what they diagnosed helped me understand the attachment dynamic that was playing out in my marriage. Without understanding this dynamic, we were constantly at odds. We were unable to control our behaviour and could not sustainably stop fighting. Learning about attachment styles was ground-breaking for me. It sounds so simple, yet when I started to work on myself using the attachment paradigm, a real shift took place in my marriage! The idea of being insecurely attached gave us a different angle to look at things. There was no more getting caught up in a whirlwind of conflict without understanding what was going on.

Having learnt about attachment, I understood that I was mostly anxiously attached to Moses. I was preoccupied with thoughts of our relationship. Strongly attracted to him, needing greater proximity and comfort. I wanted to be near him as much as possible and was in distress when we were separated even for a day. My limit was as long as it was daylight. As soon as the light in the sky would begin to fade, I would want to be around Moses. I was also extremely jealous. With the attachment lens, I started to see Moses as avoidant, generally not very expressive of emotions, did not need the same amount of proximity, protected his personal space, was easily hurt by criticism, would withdraw in conflict and his greatest fear was engulfment (being swallowed up in the marriage relationship). This was the relationship map that attachment had afforded me.

With this new lens, I started to understand our needs better. I ceased to read his actions as personal affronts and I now could understand what our fights really were about. I could not only see a consistent pattern in our conflict, but I could also predict our behaviour now. Yet understanding alone was not enough. What really changed the game was managing my insecure attachment.

Not all married people are insecurely attached. Many secure adults know how to meet their individual needs and are also amenable to meeting their spouse's needs. These marriages are not so common but they do exist. I have heard of marriages that have been stable all through. However, because we are human, there is a huge variation in marriages. We are all on a spectrum between extremely secure and extremely insecure points. Anyone can use this information of psychological attachment maps to improve their marriage.

Generally, secure people tend to attract secure partners and insecure people tend to attract insecure partners. When marriage is hard, there will usually be a degree of an insecure attachment dynamic going on with the couple.

The insecure behaviours in marriage are similar to those we mentioned in children. Anxiously attached children will be clingy, protesting separation from their primary attachment figure, and constantly seeking reassurance. Avoidantly attached children will create distance with the attachment figure and protest engulfment. Children with a disorganized attachment will show a combination of the above strategies. These same patterns that we find in children are easily observable in couples by a trained therapist and are the high drama playing itself out in marriage.

The more I practice, the more I realize that even seemingly disparate actions in a marriage can often be understood in terms of attachment dynamics. The patterns in marriage are a lot more sophisticated and that is why specialized training is required. Adults have a way of masking and modifying their real needs and sometimes an anxiously attached person appears as avoidant on the outside and it takes a practised mind to understand the convoluted behaviour. Underneath the complexity, however, are the four patterns of attachment.

Having described the invisible dynamic that is at play in marriage, you may have already started to place yourself and identify what attachment styles are manifesting in your own marriage. If you are as curious as I am, you will be eager to know which attachment style you have. Let me put you out of your misery. You can know your attachment style with a great degree of certainty in a few minutes. Use the free attachment quiz on attachment at personaldevelopmentschool.com. Just to give you a heads up: no one is 100% one style of attachment. In the past, this quiz, created by Thais Gibson, used to give you a profile showing what percentage of each style you portray. However, a more recent version will only give you your dominant attachment style. Bear in mind, though, that as humans, we do not fit neatly into the boxes of attachment style. We usually will all have a degree of other styles. However, it is helpful to know your dominant attachment style.

I find that many avoidantly attached people will answer the quiz questions in such a way that they appear secure; whereas from the clinical point of view and from the report of their spouses and their own admission, they primarily display an insecure attachment. I think this is because they have repressed emotions for long and outwardly appear in emotional control. It is likely, and this is my hypothesis, that the combination of a positive view of self and a negative view of others as well as repressed emotions makes them a little more out of touch with their emotional world than the other types. I, therefore, suggest that if you are facing relationship troubles and your result comes up as secure, just work on any insecure tendencies you notice in yourself. You will know your secondary style from your experience of relationships given the descriptions above, what your spouse tells you, and if you have a therapist that specializes in relationship psychology, they may help be able to help you too.

The reason marital troubles are so painful is that in our brains, emotional bonds are coded as a matter of life and death. In the most primitive part of our brain, a secure bond means life and an insecure bond means death. When the attachment bond is threatened, your brain sends a message saying you are in danger of physical death. This is why the breakdown of a romantic relationship can lead to several problems including suicide, the onset of mental illness, and even murders. Some people say the pain of divorce is worse than the pain of losing the loved one to death. So, the next time you experience deep pain in your romantic relationship, meet yourself with loving compassion. Know that your brain is sending you these painful signals for your own survival. However, you are not in danger of death. It is your brain's way of trying to help you survive on earth.

The wonderful news is that you can heal with or without the relationship being restored. Deep inside you, you have the memory of a secure attachment and it is possible to heal or manage this seemingly impossible pain. We call this work re-activating a secure attachment.

The attachment system is so critical to our wellbeing. That is why it is coded as a matter of life and death in our brains. It impacts how we live in this world. When one partner manages to move to a more secure stance in the relationship, the marital conflict dynamic is drastically changed! This is the good news, that you can stop the cycle of conflict by changing how you show up in the relationship! This is one of the big ideas that helped transform my marriage.

But before we get to the tools that help to manage and heal insecure attachment, let us look at other factors at play.

5

Psychological Trauma

The other thing that was a big underlying factor in my marriage was the psychological trauma that I carried into my marriage. Understanding the four attachment styles alone was not sufficient in getting us to a place of marital stability.

By trauma, I mean deep psychological/emotional wounds. According to Peter Gerlach, a therapist for over thirty-five years, 90% of the people he met in therapy had psychological wounds[1]. When trauma is mentioned, most people will think of accidents, war, rape and other such extraordinary events. In psychology, trauma practitioners now divide trauma into big 'T' trauma and little 't' trauma. The big T trauma will happen due to an incident that most people will categorize as traumatic like the aforementioned incidents, such as war, the sudden death of a close family member, rape and so on. That kind of trauma does affect us negatively. However, the trauma that dogs us most in life, and the one that is often missed in therapy is the one that is related to our attachment relationships – attachment trauma. Attachment

1 http://sfhelp.org/site/intro.htm Jan 2015

trauma happens in childhood. It is the psychological 'wound' left on a child due to events like long-term emotional neglect, low emotional nurturance, abuse, separation from one's attachment figure in times of great need. All these affect the child's ability to build strong emotional bonds with others. These wounds have a way of remaining hidden to us during our singlehood only to show up in a startling way in the intimate relationship of marriage. Gerlach outlines the symptoms of these abandonment wounds as listed below:

Six psychological wounds from early-childhood abandonment, neglect, and abuse (trauma):

1) A fragmented personality and a disabled true self. A person with a fragmented personality will have a feeling that they do not really know who they are; and feel out of touch with parts of themselves.

2) Excessive shame (low self-esteem) and excessive guilt

3) Excessive anxieties and fears of failure, criticism, rejection, abandonment, intimacy, loss of control and of the unknown

4) Difficulties with self-trust and interpersonal trust

5) Significant reality distortions such as chronic denial, minimizing, idealizing, catastrophizing, projecting, intellectualizing, and numbing

6) Difficulty feeling, bonding, empathizing, and loving.

As an adult, I became aware that I had more than a few of the above symptoms. This should not have been surprising, given the background of the sudden deaths of both of my parents at a critical stage of my development as a child. Surprisingly, I have also found these traits among couples that come to counselling even when both sets of their parents are alive. Trauma symptoms are common in my practice. I do not know whether this is because of all the trauma we have faced as a nation from political turmoil coupled with poverty that eats away at our emotional and mental health. I am writing as a Ugandan therapist that practices counselling in Uganda, but perhaps all humanity is this way, broken to some degree. Whatever the truth is, it seems trauma is lodged somewhere in our collective consciousness as a nation. In psychology, this background trauma is likely to lead to inconsistent parenting. Insufficient emotional nurturing is traumatic to a growing child and, if not addressed, will show up as a problem later on in marriage.

Most of us show up at the door of marriage with a great nurturance deficit and are desperate for love. The desperation is often not well understood by its owner let alone the unsuspecting brand-new spouse and, therefore, does not get deliberately attended to. I now see the wisdom of the Bible in saying that "a man should not go out to war for a full year after marrying his bride.[2]" Intensive nurturing is required as the first goal of marriage. This would give the couple a chance to bond emotionally.

Trauma disorganizes our ability to feel safe in the world. It creates psychological distress. A person who experiences trauma might look normal on the outside but will be anything but normal on the inside, that is, psychologically speaking. They may display signs of anxiety when there is nothing much to be anxious about, lack trust and empathy for others, quickly descend into anger and aggressive behaviour, or show sadness and general dissatisfaction with life. Unfortunately, small "t" trauma is little understood in our culture and due to the poor behaviour of small "t" trauma

---

2 See Deuteronomy 24:5

victims, relatives and friends might blame, criticize or simply push away the victim, thereby retraumatizing them.

When one does not feel psychologically safe in the world, they act selfishly. Let me give that seemingly extreme statement in the context of science. Safety in our brain is managed by two systems. There is a system that gets us ready to face danger and a system that gets us back to normal. These two systems are supposed to keep a delicate balance. Trauma knocks these systems out of balance. What happens internally when we experience trauma, is that the part of the brain responsible for survival becomes hyperactive and tends to hijack other parts of the brain. It is like an alarm system that keeps going off when there is no real danger. On the other hand, the part of the brain responsible for emotional regulation and keeping us calm becomes less active. It is supposed to switch off the proverbial alarm but it does not. So, the alarm stays on too long, sending the message, "You are in danger! You are in danger!" when, in fact, you are not. This imbalance is reflected in the emotional turmoil of people that have experienced trauma. Too much energy is spent on scanning the environment for danger. This constant suspicion that things are going to go wrong leads to the emotional system being overloaded. Victims of trauma may end up having a lower tolerance for most disturbances. Their resilience is eaten up by the two malfunctioning systems. The person is in a state of hypervigilance for too long and experiences high levels of stress. So, when a victim of trauma acts selfishly, it is that they are in survival mode most of the time. The loving side of their brain is hijacked by the survival side. They do not consciously choose to be selfish but are locked out of a large part of their potential to be kind and fully human. Unfortunately, if this persistent stress goes on for too long, it creates personality deficits and disease.

Most people who do not get appropriate attention after a traumatic incident will find ways of coping with the emotional turmoil that defines their lives. They may develop addictions, both substance and behavioural, including alcohol, sex, drugs, overworking, eating disorders, extreme discipline in sports and religious fanaticism. Also, these individuals may express higher levels of anxiety, depression or suicide.

Trauma can be occasioned on a person by their loved one. Behaviours such as extreme emotional neglect, domestic violence, infidelity, verbal and sexual abuse, physical and financial abandonment, are all commonly found in marriage. If, for example, a wife was frightened to have a C-section at delivery and desperately wanted to have her husband at her side in the hospital and he did not show up, the wife may experience this as a trauma. A more extreme example is experiencing continuous verbal or physical abuse from a loved one; this too can lead to trauma.

More often than not, most adults will have experienced several little 't' traumas but also some big 'T' traumas. Certainly, those of us who grew up in Uganda in the 1970s have lived through a few wars and civil unrest. Many of us lost our loved ones to the wars, brutal regimes and the chaos that goes along with a poorly run country. During those times, poverty and crime rates were high. For many of us, either we or people close to us have experienced terrible situations. Just being a witness to the trauma of a loved one induces stress. This stress is real and also has an impact on our ability to feel safe in the world. This stress can be transmitted to the next generation. One of the ways that it is transmitted to the next generation is through the attachment system.

When parents carry untreated trauma, their ability to form strong emotional bonds with their children is affected. They are likely to emotionally neglect their children due to the high levels of internal stress they carry, thereby creating insecure attachment bonds with their children. What is more, they may have developed some distorted views of the world like "The world is an unsafe place," and are likely to pass on these beliefs to their children. They do not do this consciously but subconsciously. The poor emotional regulation of traumatized parents, in turn, traumatizes children. These parents will often have strong anger outbursts, or swing to the other extreme and fail to meaningfully engage emotionally. This is how the cycle passes on from generation to generation.

There is a degree of trauma in every population. I believe this factor is affecting us as a people generally. Psychological services are not a priority in a population where many people are simply trying to survive; let alone the more specialized trauma counselling that effectively reduces trauma symptoms. As a result, many people walk around with undiagnosed and untreated trauma, it is not a surprise when the problems of untreated trauma show up in marriages.

Lois Ochieng, one of Uganda's leading trauma therapists, cites some symptoms of trauma as "hyperarousal; jumpiness; sharpened senses; fast heartbeat; chronic pain or recurring injuries; sensitivities and intolerances to foods and chemicals; avoidance of emotions; strong startle response to unexpected touch, sound or light; suicidal feelings; finding challenges in executing basic self-care like laundry, meals, etc; a fiercely critical internal voice; consistent shallow breathing from the chest rather than the belly; flashbacks or re-experiencing a traumatic event through the senses (hearing, sight or emotions)." Looking back at my experience of life before trauma therapy, I see that untreated trauma made me highly negative and aggressive. I carried a constant worry that something would go wrong and I thought this was how life was for everyone. I also suffered low energy for a long time.

To understand trauma, let us liken the human brain to a computer. We input letters by typing into this computer. These letters form words, which form sentences and documents. We then label these documents and file them in an order that makes sense. Having order or a system for filing information, facilitates later retrieval of these documents whenever we need them. Likewise, our minds take in pictures, sounds and smells, and combine these pieces of data to make files that are our memories. These help us to develop blueprints to interpret life in the future. For example, when you see a green flat oval with a tiny handle, your brain quickly tells you it is a leaf. You might even decide it is a leaf you can eat like a lettuce leaf. Pictures, sizes and uses of objects have been stored in your brain and are retrieved for use when needed. This retrieval happens in split seconds. However, when trauma happens, we often fail to put the particular fragments of data, for example, the angry words and horrific images, into a cohesive "document". Ochieng says that unlike other memories that are stored in our minds as stories, trauma is stored in our mind and body as fragments of information, like visual images, smells, sounds, tastes or touch. We are therefore unable to put away the information. The loose bits of information scatter around our filing system and start to create system glitches. Most of this happens in the deep recesses of the proverbial 'computer' and is not immediately obvious to the user since he or she is able to pull up a number of other files that seem to work pretty well. The system glitches are all the above signs and symptoms I have mentioned. They are usually unexplained strong negative reactions to a varied range of stimuli. For example, developing a feeling of disgust to a seemingly innocuous sound or smell, easily startling at sounds, etc.

In the past, it was thought that psychological trauma could not be cured. However, with the new treatments that have emerged, that idea is debatable. One of the older treatments for trauma that has been utilized over the years, focuses on increasing exposure to the negative stimulus in order to reduce the negative reaction. This treatment, called exposure therapy, is given in the hope that repeated exposure to the stimulus will desensitize a person from the stimulus and diminish or extinguish the extreme negative reactions. For example, if you jump every time you see a shoelace, thinking it is a snake, you might want to have an intentional routine where you play with shoelaces to cause your system to recognize that they are harmless.

There are many other trauma treatments. One that particularly interests me is EMDR (Eye Movement Desensitization Reprocessing). This is a newer therapy that I am happy to announce is available in Uganda. It is more selective with which parts of trauma it re-exposes the client to, with an intention to help the brain reprocess the memory more cohesively and develop new, more adaptive interpretations of what happened.

Let me continue to tell you my story. Perhaps you will now see clearly the patterns of attachment insecurity and trauma symptoms combined in it.

In attachment language, what characterized our marriage was my feelings of abandonment as an anxiously attached wife. I would then reach for Moses, at first gently, but then eventually more and more aggressively. Eventually, I would grow angry and attack him for being inconsiderate. He, on the other hand, was so scared by my anger and, as an avoidant partner, felt his autonomy was under attack. He had grown up self-supporting and did not know why I was so upset about spending time on my own and why I was so angry at him. Anxious partners will tend to express their abandonment distress through anger while avoidant partners tend to express their distress by withdrawing.

The more I attacked, the more Moses withdrew. His withdrawal had the effect of making me feel even more abandoned. He ran a really busy life and worked thirteen-hour days most weekdays. My protestations increased to the level where I was angry most times.

My anger led to nit-picking. I could go off about anything. He, on the other hand, would withdraw when I was angry and would not engage in the quarrel most times. He would ask me to postpone our discussions (a typical stance of avoidance). He was feeling both attacked and degraded by my tone of voice and anger. What Moses was doing as an avoidant was creating distance and avoiding conflict.

Moses' silence was troubling to me. My brain system would be triggered to abandonment. I was even more frightened by silence, but I was not aware that under my anger was a real fear of abandonment. What I was aware of was that his behaviour made me really angry.

Conversely, my anger was unbearable and felt very threatening to Moses. Moses felt that his autonomy was being attacked and he would protect it by stonewalling (refusing to respond). He also hoped that if he did not respond to my anger then I would calm down. Needless to say, this was an erroneous assumption.

This became our cycle – me pursuing and criticizing Moses and him withdrawing from me. His withdrawal made me panic and go after him even more aggressively and my aggression frightened him and made him withdraw even more. We were scaring each other a lot! We cycled around in conflict for so long that I thought we might never make it.

I guess this dynamic of an unhappy cycle of fighting is what the sengas were going on about before I was married. The pattern is predictable. The presenting issues can be different: lack of finances or failure to share them, in-law issues, lack of romance, infidelity, infertility, you name it. Underlying these fights, though, is always that dynamic where one partner is demanding and the other one not showing up to meet that demand, but instead creates distance. On close examination, a milder version of the attachment cycle of conflict may be at play even in healthy marriages.

We tried therapy, read and exchanged many books, brought in advisers and attended various marriage courses. Sometimes it felt as if we were making progress, but then we usually just cycled back around the same issues. Sometimes I was discouraged enough to give up and then other times I was ready to fight.

Earlier in our marriage, I learnt a lot from marriage fellowships. However, as our marriage advanced in years, we found that the marriage fellowships' advice was mostly for early marriage years and the solutions were not deep enough. The topics were often repetitive and superficial. For example, I had never heard of attachment styles and psychological trauma as topics in marital groups. This led me to books and the internet. I started to hear speakers on the internet that were describing our relationship without ever having met us. One of these specialists was Dr. Doug Weiss. He described what I was experiencing: I was married but felt alone! He described my experience in detail without ever having met me! For me, this was a spectacular find!

I knew I was onto something. I started to feel optimistic. I was amazed at the way he organized and categorized the types of marriage failures. If he and other specialists were able to accurately describe the problems, then it was likely that they had accurately found the solutions as well. This set me up on a quest to find the solutions.

In the meantime, we sought marriage therapy in Uganda a few times. The pastoral therapy was the most helpful. We felt loved by our pastors and it also gave us a place for accountability. Love and accountability were good ingredients for hope. We saw glimpses of improvement but we usually did not manage to sustain the change interventions. I also did not feel that we ever got a good grasp of everything that was going on with us. Something fundamental was missing in our therapy. I did not know what it was. I felt a certain lack of clarity. However, the experts on YouTube had clearer analyses of the possible causes of our marital problems. I was slowly picking up a new language from these experts. A language that helped me put words to what I was experiencing; a language that validated my experience. The more I researched, the more I was convinced that there were answers out there that we had never heard of. I was filled with hope. This hope created a shift in me.

The speakers that really had solutions were mostly in the US. Not one to be daunted by impossible ideas, I started to nurse the idea of going abroad to find answers to my questions. I knew they were out there, particularly in the US. I wanted to go to the US not only to study, but I felt that I still had a wounded heart from my childhood and needed a kind of therapy I had not yet received. (This was the trauma of losing my parents. I did not understand, but felt things were not quite right inside).

I picked up the phone and rang Dr. Doug Weiss' office. I booked a slot in the hope that I would be able to convince Moses, but he was unresponsive when I pitched this idea. I did not succeed in convincing him. I could not justify the cost of extensive therapy in Uganda or in the US – it was not a thing that was done, especially since I could not prove that it would help. But I knew I needed more. I also could not justify to myself spending whatever money I needed to go abroad for therapy and so I put this idea on the back burner.

An idea that started to form in my mind was that of further education. I love knowledge and I love to learn. I reasoned that if I was going to study further, why not take on a field that already interested me. With hindsight, I realize that although I could not justify to myself spending a large sum of money on therapy then, I could justify to myself a colossal sum for an education; and spending money on education is more acceptable in the Ugandan culture.

Moses was not against the idea of studying further. In fact, he had always encouraged me to study further as a backup plan in case he died prematurely (like my parents and his dad had) and was not able to look after me. I tried talking him into coming with me to the US, but always the practical one, he could not see how we could survive on a student visa that would not allow him paid work. How would he support the family? He was right. I had no idea how we would survive without his income. He encouraged me to apply for admission to a university of my liking and we would figure it out in time. We talked it over with elders we both respect in our family, and they too gave their blessing.

But how would I go away from my family as a woman, leaving my husband alone? It was just not done! I was plagued by doubt made worse by some people brave enough to tell me to my face that I would lose my husband to a mistress. I was told scary stories of other families around this theme. I often did not have a rebuttal. All I knew was that this was the next logical step. Inside me, my inner knower was not afraid to take this step. However, it took a lot of courage for me to take it. I am so glad I did because now we have reaped the benefits of finding answers and I am here to share with you the solutions.

Now let us get to the steps of the work of building a more secure attachment style. The steps I took to transform my marriage.

6

The Marriage Makeover

I would not be sharing all these things except that I have seen undeniable results of taking this journey. I have and continue to work on a total transformation of my marriage and have experienced a great shift. Peace has come to our home and for that, I am so thankful. The conflict cycle has ended and I want to share my knowledge and experience so you too can benefit from it. Below I will share the "lessons" I learnt sequentially (more or less) to a more fulfilling marriage. Each lesson took me several months to learn and I am still circling back to some of the lessons.

Lesson 1: Deciding that a stale marriage was not for me and believing for more

As humans, we mostly do not like change. As long as our discomfort is tolerable, most of us will not be motivated to do things differently. In my marriage, when Moses and I were in conflict, we tried small efforts here and there to change but did not really follow through. I had to get properly fed up before making the decision that I did not like what I had and that I wanted more. Decision making started the journey in earnest for us.

Before the firm decision to change, I got to a place where it seemed so pointless to fight. Nothing I said was making a sustainable difference. Any changes we made were short-lived. I was stumped! I came to that place where I did not even have any more fight left in me. I was silent. I am not the type to give up a fight I believe in. I either win or die trying. I was tempted to give up. But I eventually got to a point of mentally giving myself an ultimatum. I had only two options: to quit or to do something about our situation. I opted to do something and I was prepared to do it, if not together, then alone.

Looking back, I realize this was an important first step. I refused to be satisfied with the way things were. I became seized by the idea that things could be different. I became resolute about fighting for my marriage, I decided to do something big about it. This is what led to all the wonderful changes we have seen. Refusing to be satisfied led me to acknowledge my deep desire for a better marriage. I believe our passion for life is always alive at our core and leads us to a fuller life. As divine beings, we are blessed with the ability to believe that things can change for the better, regardless of our circumstances. That belief, no matter how misguided it may sound, changes the future and makes things happen.

This was all that was needed for help to start finding me. I started to get new insights. I was reading a lot about our problems and suddenly a new body of knowledge started to unfold to me. Sometimes I have wondered why this knowledge was not availed to us before. These new insights gave me a lot of hope, but perhaps it is the other way round; maybe it is hope that gave me the new insights. This refusal to settle, combined with a hunger for more, coupled with research to understand the issue better, is an approach I use to solve most problems, whether it is raising a child, planting a forest or learning to cook Chinese food. I yearn for more, research and read around it.

I could have decided to tolerate my marriage. I could have bought into the idea that this was all marriage was meant to be. However, I refused to be satisfied and settle for a poor marriage. I found it unacceptable and that was when I decided to do something about it.

Lesson 2: Trusting that I would be okay

If you had asked me what I hoped for our marriage, my initial dreams had died and I did not really have a vision of the future. The vision I was able to work on was one of my personal happiness and it turns out, that was a reasonable place to start.

This picture of my future started to become concrete when I asked myself two critical questions: If Moses did not change, what would I do with my life? Could I be happy? At this stage, I was convinced he was the one that needed to change. Wrong view but great question.

One day, in answer to these questions, I pictured myself in a brightly lit room at a university in a foreign country, in a beautiful apartment with white walls and colourful wall hangings of green vegetation. I was completely at peace in this picture and in charge of my life. Moses would visit me in this picture and we were closer and in a better state of friendship. The picture that came to my mind made me feel so safe and happy that I started to use it regularly. I was practising trust and peace in the middle of my circumstances.

Then I started to think about what else it was that I was supposed to be doing with my life. I love knowledge and my favourite thing to do is to learn new things. Moses had always wanted me to study further. I had always wanted to have a stint abroad. So, my mind came up with a creative solution. The idea was to pursue a master's degree abroad. I would acquire new, exciting knowledge in the area of counselling psychology and get to also live overseas (I had always wanted this as a child). Trusting that I would be okay in the end opened my mind up to this creative solution.

Lesson 3: Finding meaning in the negatives of life

At about that time of decision making, I was encouraged to read a book by Dr. J. Robert Clinton titled *The Making of a Leader.* In it, I found a section about negative preparation. I had never heard the term before. What on earth was negative preparation? Within a few paragraphs, I understood that these were the difficulties in our lives that mould who we become. The hardships that become the main propellants towards a certain direction. Hardships that lead us to our calling! Whereas I had always had an interest in marriage and marital counselling, I had not chosen to have marital troubles. Yet it was the marital troubles that were motivating me to take the deep dive of studying couple, marriage and family counselling at a master's level, at the best possible institution that was within my reach. My previous interest had been insufficient to get me into any concrete training. Without our troubles, I would have been reluctant to take a step like this. If this was how God got me to do what he wanted me to do, I was game. I felt that this message on 'negative preparation' was from God directly to me. Have you ever had that feeling? That a message was divine? Well, I kept this message in my heart.

At this time, I also visited a church called Worship Harvest near my home where they had started the Bible sermon series on Joseph and his dream. I returned every week to this church primarily to complete this sermon series. The message, in a nutshell, was that God can give and guide you to achieve a seemingly impossible dream. Once again, I felt this was no coincidence. I was so energized each week by these sermons. For me, it was God personally speaking to my situation. When I would sit under these sermons, a warm feeling would come over my chest and a feeling of joy would fill me. I felt inspired. With hindsight, the Bible says in Hebrews 11:1, "Faith is the substance of things hoped for, the evidence of things not seen." The substance, "tangible material", were the emotions of confident excitement and joy that were forming inside me concerning my dream. On the outside, I looked the same, yet on the inside, I had taken hold of something exciting. The joy I felt was as if I had already taken hold of the future!

Yet not everything was simple. I too had my doubts. Was I right to go against the culture to leave my husband for 'studies'? On some level, I was afraid and confused. If this was God's will for me, why were things not working out smoothly? But at my core, I was convinced of my mission and I was resolute. The truth was, at my core, I was filled with more courage than fear. Yet if I allowed my brain to overthink things, I became afraid. If we were going to have a marriage at all, it needed to be a proper marriage, not one driven by fear, but by two willing partners. When my doubts would arise, I would beg Moses to go with Plan A, which was to go for this intensive therapy for a week or else for him to seek a position abroad so that I would be with him. This I could easily picture. But he said he wanted for me to find the university, apply and settle and he would be following me this time. I had always followed him.

I ended up zeroing in on a Master's program in Marital and Family Counselling at Regent University in Virginia Beach, Virginia, USA. I had no idea where the funding would come from. I wrote down a list of seventeen things that needed to happen for me to pull off this herculean idea. I focused on only a few tasks at a time. I was as surprised as anyone when those tasks kept getting ticked off.

Within eight months, I had an admission, a visa in hand and tuition for one year. I was unbelieving still, in a sort of daze. Initially, we had planned that our son Tal, would stay with Moses in Uganda. Along the way, though, Tal decided that he wanted to try out the football opportunities in the US and that he would come with me. I was pleased that he had come to this decision by himself.

On the 5th of January 2018, we went as a small party of six close family members to Entebbe airport. As we stood at Departures, it was time to say goodbye. A sob erupted from somewhere inside of me as I hugged my sister and then Moses. It was a hard parting. I felt unsure about the wisdom of my move, but at a certain level, I was filled with courage and boldness. Our travel also happened amidst the worst winter storm Virginia had experienced in twenty years. I was both frightened and excited. I was open to whatever lay ahead.

I quickly settled into my classes. I did not waste my studies in Family Therapy. I was there to find solutions and so I was super engaged in those classes. I had questions for me and for all the couples that I left in Uganda. The university provided both psychological and counselling services as well as career guidance, professional mentorship and pastoral services free to students and I took the opportunity to utilize all these services. I also regularly received pastoral ministry at Azalea Garden Church which was a walking distance from my university. If they made an altar call for anything remotely related to my situation, I was not shy about it; I went to the altar. If they asked us to write down prayer requests,

I filled my form and asked for prayer. In addition, I kept applying the strategies that I was learning in my classes on myself and my family.

Moses rang Tal and me most days at 2 pm after we got off work and school and I used this time to share my latest gleanings. I attacked small problems and big problems and found that I was finding success. I decided then that I was going to identify the strategies that were working and make them available to the world.

Lesson 4: Clarifying the destination

One cannot devise a plan to reach a destination that remains undefined. I needed to change my marriage, but I was not sure what the specifics of my destination were. One of the simple yet revolutionary ideas I picked up in my studies was that one of the main purposes of family was for people to meet each other's emotional needs. In marriage preparation courses, even the ones I have taught in the past, we are usually taught all about the physical, perhaps even the social, sexual and spiritual needs; but I have not been to a training where we are comprehensively taught how to understand and meet each other's emotional needs. Emotional needs started to come out as the area I needed to focus on.

In order not to throw out the baby (the other good areas of marriage we already emphasise) with the bathwater, I will share a helpful way to remember marital and family needs holistically. This is with Dr. Spirit's five compatibility needs which follow an acronym **RISES**: **R**ecreational, **I**ntellectual, **S**piritual, **E**motional, and **S**exual. Since there are many good books on all the other areas, I will spend much of the rest of this book focusing on understanding and meeting emotional needs individually and as a couple.

A great part of who we are as humans is simply this: that we are bonding creatures. In marriage and family, this is the real crux of the matter, the part that holds all the other parts together. This is why the attachment theory is revolutionary. Human behaviour makes so much sense once you grasp the attachment theory. Emotional needs were not on my radar in a concrete way previously. So my failure to succeed in this area should not have been surprising. I had this idea, I guess from romantic movies, that living together blissfully forever was easy and I longed for that. I had hoped that things would sort themselves out, but the truth was that I had no understanding of what things made up the bliss that I longed for, let alone have the tools or strategies to reach my ideal marriage.

Looking back at the early years of our marriage, it was clear that we had elaborate goals to meet our financial and material needs, but we had little in the way of clear goals about our emotional needs. Through my training, I assessed our marriage and decided that we needed to work on our emotional bonding. Science shows that if a couple will build a strong emotional bond, they will be able to solve most of their other problems. I, therefore, developed a goal of emotional intimacy for my marriage. Hoping was not enough; we had to know what to do and work towards it intentionally. Clarifying my destination as a strong emotional bond was, therefore, an important step in my journey. I agree with this quote by Chuck Blakeman: "In life, you get what you intend, not what you hope for."

My hope is that by this point in the book, you and your spouse have taken the attachment quiz and decided that you want more. Now, commit to figuring out how to form a mutually satisfying emotional and spiritual bond, also known as a secure attachment. This is the best destination for any marriage!

Lesson 5: It is not about you!

This lesson came to me in 2017, after I had applied to the universities in the US for further studies, and before I was admitted, I heard about a two-week training for Christian counsellors called Living Wisdom. The course is developed and written by David Riddell, a New Zealander, and had run a couple of sessions in previous years at Makindye Country Club in Uganda. Lucky for me, the year I was ready, David Riddell, the originator of the course himself, would be presenting most of the sessions and boy, was he something! He was deeply insightful and full of wisdom and had a way of distilling complex issues into some basic categories. Not only that, I fell in love with Living Wisdom because it has simple, practical interventions. Living Wisdom is a combination of three types of therapy and Biblical understandings.

The main therapeutic influence in Living Wisdom is a therapy called CBT (Cognitive Behavioural Therapy). In it lies the idea that "our thoughts, emotions, self-talk (the things we tell ourselves) and our behaviour are interlinked." So interventions at different parts of our thought-behaviour chain will change our experience of life. Thoughts can change emotions, emotions can change behaviour, self-talk can change behaviour and behaviour can change emotions and so on and so forth. In Living Wisdom, we were taught to observe, monitor and change our thoughts. One of the common types of faulty thinking is the self-referential interpretation of others' behaviour. In other words, thinking that "what people do is about me". For example, if I enter a room and someone else walks out, faulty thinking would say, "That person does not like me." CBT suggests that thinking like that causes a lot of emotional problems.

A more helpful way of viewing the same pattern is this: there could be any number of reasons a person walks out of a room at the time you entered it. They might have needed to go to the bathroom. Or perhaps they needed to take a call. So, to teach us healthier thinking, in his opening session, David Riddell said there was an attitude crucial to living with wisdom in life. The attitude is summed up by the words, "It is not about you," which simply means that what people do to you is often not about you. Try and find other ways of interpreting behaviour and you will live a much happier life. Married couples in conflict will usually interpret their spouse's behaviour as being about them. It is not uncommon to find that one or both partners are deeply offended.

Choosing to take offence implies that you think they are doing this intentionally against you. When you understand that people's behaviour is more often about the story of their own lives than it is about you, you take less and less offence. One of the ways therapy is conducted is to lend the client a new way of looking at the issues in their lives. "It is not about you" has been one really helpful perspective.

For instance, when Moses and I attended a marriage course one time, Moses found that the men in his group were complaining about criticism from their wives, the same thing as he was facing with me. He was surprised that other women in Kampala were just like me. He realized then that this behaviour that seemed very targeted at him was not me uniquely finding a way to rankle him, but it was quite common in marriage. This gave him a change in perspective. "If the conflict cycles were identical in other couples like us, then something else must be at play," he thought. This also meant that if either of us went and got a new spouse, we would likely end up with a change of spouse but the same problems.

It really was not about us. Maybe it was something in the Kampala food, or air that caused women to be critical because it seemed like a plague. Whatever it was, Moses was heartened to find that it was not about him.

So, if your husband does not call you to tell you he is running late, and you sit there fuming not because he is late, but because you feel like you are not a priority, remember, it is not about you! If your wife constantly nags you about small things and seems to always find fault with you, don't take things too personally. It is not about you. The criticising and nagging wife is not only found in Kampala, she is even mentioned in the Bible. The dominating or insensitive husband is thousands of years old. What you are dealing with is not a personal attack, even though it might look like it. So, next time your spouse acts unlovingly, tell yourself that it is not about you. It is a relational programme playing. Psychology tells us that most of our programmes were set up in childhood. This is the time we are most programmable. So, the programme predates marriage.

It was easy for me to implement this thinking in other relationships. I learnt to tell myself it really is not about me. Perhaps the person in question was having a bad day, week, year or even life; I let them off the hook that way. It was hard, at first, to apply this attitude in my marriage. I found that I had learnt quite quickly to find more helpful ways of interpreting the behaviour of friends and family. It was not as fast, though, to work this learning into my marriage. I guess it is because Moses, as an intimate partner, is in a different category in my mind with different expectations of behaviour. I suspect that the level of attachment to a person matters in learning this attitude. But I definitely learnt to offer more grace.

Side note: In case you are reading this book and you are yet to find a partner, here is a tip for you. You may be wondering how to choose someone that is emotionally healthy. Well, one of the biggest indicators of poor emotional/relational programming is taking offence easily. It is an indicator that ones' emotional programme may be out of sync. "It is normal to take offence once in a while. But it is another to always be gravely offended," David Riddell says, "A person who takes offence easily communicates that they are not okay. Since they are not okay, they are going to make it hard for everyone around them. They will question every motive and intention of the people around them. Unfortunately, they are not going to be reliable in their assessment of others. Through the lens of their own self-rejection, they will always perceive others as rejecting them." Such a person can address the underlying factor with a trained therapist.

The Drama stage in marriage has a lot to do with couples being offended by each other. They cannot conceive how their spouse's actions are not about them. Which other way of seeing the world is there except a view of self? They have arrived at very painful conclusions like, "I am unloved by my spouse", "I am unappreciated", "I cannot make her happy", and "Something is wrong with me or she would like me". These awful thoughts are held subconsciously and cause a lot of pain for the couple. It is easy to feel hurt by someone when you think they do not love you or think that there is something wrong with you. These thoughts act as a background belief that is then used to interpret behaviour. A terribly warped story of one's spouse ensues out of this thinking mess.

As Moses worked harder and harder, I drew up a story about him. What in our story was a loving husband (Moses) working hard to end poverty in his immediate and extended family and making every possible sacrifice so that his family would never lack even if he died prematurely, became the story of a neglectful husband who did not care about his wife and spent all his time at work, trying to get ahead in his career that he loved more than her!

It was all clear to me. Of course, I was right. I was not open to any other ways of interpreting his behaviour and my warped mind continued to find evidence to confirm my conclusion.

Whereas there are faulty ways of thinking that are common to most couples, one will find slight changes in the details of the wrong thinking. In this book, I may not help you uncover which wrong belief you have swallowed, but suffice it to say at this stage that it is not about you. Your spouse's failure to act lovingly toward you is not about you. Don't take it so personally. One day you will understand that there is more to the behaviour than meets the eye. The drunken lover is a child locked in grief over the past, the bitter woman is in pain over some trauma, and so on. Your spouse's actions do not determine your worth nor your enjoyment of life. You have to find a more reliable indicator of your worth than your spouse's behaviour.

Lesson 6: Being more assertive (please note, there is a difference between assertiveness and aggression)

At the same Living Wisdom training, I learnt a lot about assertiveness and boundaries. There were many rules that I had been given as a woman in marriage under the lessons of submission in both my ethnic and Christian cultures. I may have misunderstood the lessons but I realized that I was often showing up as less than Moses to discussions, and to decisions. I assumed I was less intelligent, less analytical and less knowledgeable, and so I hung back on my true thoughts and gave in to decisions I did not entirely agree with. I had thought that this is what submission meant. I was not in agreement about a lot of ways that we ran our family and I was in several "pretend" agreements.

In Living Wisdom, we were encouraged to stop all pretend agreements. So, I challenged myself to live up to the Bible verse which says, "Let your yes be yes and your no be no." This was a choice to become more authentic, more engaged and bring more of myself to the table. I was going to stop being nice outwardly and resentful inside. I determined to be really honest. If I said yes, I was really agreed and if I did not agree, I was going to be honest and say so and even if I let Moses make the decision in his favour, I was going to be clear and communicate what I thought and give my reasons. It was a kind of assertiveness that I had in me all along but often neglected. It really felt good to be assertive. I felt more in harmony on the inside. Who I was inside did not have to be hidden or masked. In that time, for example, I turned down a couple of family events that I felt were overly burdensome to me and opted to do things I enjoyed instead. The next time those events happened, we set them up in a way that I could also enjoy them.

Lesson 7: The only person you can change is you

My second therapist in the US was a kind, portly man that was both gentle and astute in counselling. He was humble enough to not assume marriage worked the same way in Uganda as it did in the US. He would ask me how things worked in a Ugandan marriage so that he could appropriately support me. I felt that my culture was respected and this also gave me a chance to review what my individual culture was. Even though he was that humble, he did not shy away from challenging me on some other issues when I was being stubborn and did not want to change. He was soft and firm at the same time. I was later surprised to discover that he was about my age; because he was a very knowledgeable and skilled therapist, I had assumed he was much older.

He practised reality therapy and one of its main tenets is, "The only person you can change is you." I had a list of things I wanted to be changed in my marriage and I thought that most of the change would have to be made by Moses. However, my therapist kept bringing me back to this principle. I was not allowed to have any fantasy about my husband changing. He might never change. That was a hard pill for me to swallow because I erroneously believed that if Moses loved me just the way I needed to be loved, I would transform into the sweet wife he always wanted.

My therapist made it clear that he was not going to work on my marriage with my husband thousands of miles away. He said there was no way we could conduct marital therapy with just one person. This was a solid/sound stance for me. It lowered my expectations. Even in this individual therapy, he had to keep reminding me that the only person I could change was myself. Even if my husband was available for therapy, I could never change him. The only option available to me was to change myself.

After a while, this message sank in and I started to work on myself and take control of my life. It was up to me to remain unchanged and tolerate the marriage, or work on myself. The only option that was not on the table was asking my spouse to change. Blaming Moses was a way of playing the victim. Stopping to blame him, therefore, meant that I had to move from the victim position to being fully engaged with my life. If I wanted anything to change, I would have to take action. All options were on the table for me, the only one not available was blaming. I was going to work at it without waiting for my husband to rescue me. This blame game thing was one of the hardest behaviours for me to break. It turns out I was so well practised it was second nature to me. I blamed effortlessly. So, taking responsibility for how I am faring in marriage is a skill I have had to learn.

Looking back now, this was another crucial lesson on my journey as an individual and on our journey as a couple. I had to learn to show up in the marriage not as a helpless victim but as a person who could make choices. I had agency and I was going to use it. If we were having trouble, I had to choose to either be a victim and sit and complain or to do something about it. This meant that I stopped hiding behind Moses. I was not a child anymore. I started to really examine my life. What did I want out of it? What could I control? It turned out I could control a lot! So, I went about doing just that.

I started to make small adjustments to my life in order to achieve what it is that I really want out of life. I started to make life more satisfactory to me, bit by bit. This did not take away our fights in a day, but it did refocus my energy in a new way. Instead of focusing on changing Moses, I was getting to work on my life. It was a seesaw at first. I would stop fighting and throw myself into working on myself and my new pursuits and then swing back with all sorts of accusations that boil down to "Why don't you make me happy?" With time, the incremental adjustments started to provide dividends and so much good started to come to me. My life was changing and, surprisingly, so was my marriage!

Looking back now, my therapist was both right and wrong. He was right to advise me as he did, but working on myself meant that I was showing up as a different person in the marriage and later I found that this changed Moses' attitude towards me.

Lesson 8: First aid (Seven habits that improve mental health)

That same therapist in Virginia introduced me to a list of basic mental health habits. He told me there were practices that he gave each client of his as first aid. At the time, he did not explain why he put me on these practices. Along the way, I have learnt the reason why these practices are important so let me give you some context to them.

The brain is responsible for your attachment style. So, you need to be able to manage your brain health as part of your strategy for a strong marriage. Just like you wouldn't load expensive software on a broken computer, attachment work is best done in a healthy brain. Brain and mental health is perhaps the most important preparation for recovery of relationships. A healthy brain will create a more stable personality and therefore healthier relationships. A return to health can only be achieved through intentional work.

When my therapist shared this list, I realized that I had come across it on YouTube during my many searches before my studies in the US. The presenter on YouTube had been Dr Stephen Ilardi of Kansas University, an expert in treating depression. He has extensively studied brain function and says that the modern lifestyle we lead is really against brain and mental health. To quote him, "We were never designed for the sedentary, indoor, sleep-deprived, socially-isolated, fast-food-laden, frenetic pace of modern life." The brain is the control centre for the entire body, telling different parts of the body to repair, grow, get rid of unwanted material. So, it is highly important that the brain is given enough nutrients and breaks to do its very important work! This work includes storage of memories, processing events of the day and switching genes on and off, and really needs to be looked after. Dr. Ilardi designed a set of habits that he called 'The Therapeutic Lifestyle'. My therapist's list was almost identical to this and it had the following recommendations.

Have regular sleep of seven to nine hours. As the first step to relationship recovery, start to sleep at a good hour well before midnight and try to wake up at the same time daily. This helps to establish a good long sleep cycle. The reason we are told to sleep well before midnight is that science teaches us that getting good long sleep at night is more refreshing than snatches of sleep during the day, even if these snatches of sleep combined are equal in duration to the night sleep. Don't wait to get overly tired. Just train yourself to sleep. Most people I know are sleep deprived and often wear this fact as a badge of honour. What they may not know is that brain scans of people that are sleep deprived show a significant difference from those who are not. To me, the images look like the brains are filled with potholes! By the time the brain takes on physical characteristics due to a lack of sleep, just imagine how much function is actually affected prior to its showing physical deformities?

Poor sleep impacts your ability to focus, make decisions, generate a good mood and lots more. All this affects how you show up in relationships. When we lie down horizontally to sleep, we increase the amount of blood circulating in our brain, and we also allow the brain (the most complex computer on earth) to work on its filing (memory) system. This filing away of bits of information is necessary to maintain optimum functioning and access to correct files when you want them A lifestyle of sleep deprivation is also associated with emotional detachment, higher stress levels in the body, early onset of Alzheimer's, obesity, diabetes, and many more diseases. In the long run, it does not pay off. So, a small change to give yourself a fighting chance in the marriage is to start to get adequate sleep.

Take small breaks in your workday. The brain is similar to a computer and taking small breaks prevents your brain from accumulating stress. Just like any computer, if you keep giving it commands all day, at some point, the computer starts freezing. Your brain needs those frequent breaks. They do not have to be long – maybe five minutes every hour. Do this regularly and see the difference in your stress levels in just two weeks. I call these 'mini vacations' and put some effort into mine. I love the outdoors and I love nature. So, I take breaks to stretch and observe birds, flowers and plants and return refreshed. Use these small breaks to also stretch your body. Stretching reduces stress and is an excellent use of break times. Stretching is therapeutic in and of itself. It improves blood circulation and body function. It also reduces tension, thereby improving mood.

Drink enough water. Your weight in kilograms divided by 30 is the water you need to drink daily in litres. So, for example, if you are 60 kg, 60 divided by 30 is 2. Therefore, you would need to drink two litres of water daily. Your brain is made up of cells and for these cells to function properly, they need a good amount of hydration. Dehydration slows down the brain. I have heard it said that we can greatly reduce the number of people that are depressed and anxious just by eliminating dehydration. A life hack that was passed on to me from one of my best buddies is, "Buy a water bottle that you can move around with and that will enable you to sip water all through the day." This has worked for me and for many people I know because the water is always in easy reach.

Eat a balanced diet of fruits, vegetables and proteins. My therapist told me to eat my meals regularly, ensuring that I ate a balanced diet that included fruits and vegetables and to cut down on sugar, alcohol and caffeine. In most Ugandan cultures, carbohydrates are eaten in bulk and it is easy to think we are well fed. However, if we load our bodies with carbohydrates, they break down into sugars that we might not want. We do need carbohydrates but in moderation. Some micronutrients are specifically found in fruits and vegetables that support mental health. Research shows that depression and anxiety are inversely related to a good diet of fruits and vegetables. I even encourage a visit to the doctors to run blood tests for various micronutrients. It is said that once you are depleted of most micronutrients, you usually cannot make up the deficit by diet alone, but need supplements to help you restore normal levels before you can then maintain these levels by diet. It is not uncommon for people to get vitamin D, B or C supplements and find that their mood and general well-being improve greatly, saving them several quarrels with their spouse and months of therapy. As for excessive sugar, alcohol and caffeine, these three substances are potentially addictive and affect the level of stimulation of the brain as well as impact how messages are passed on in our nerves. They are best used in moderation, but can also be eliminated.

Exercise outdoors. Dr. Stephen Ilardi says, "If exercise was a pill, it would be the most effective antidepressant that has ever existed in history." Additional research shows that exercise improves self-esteem and the general functioning of the brain. Other studies on happiness reveal that being outdoors for twenty minutes daily, especially in green spaces, increases happiness. So why not kill two birds with one stone by getting your exercise outdoors? In Uganda, the weather is almost always lovely. The sun on your skin gives you vitamin D which also makes you feel happier and all this is free. If you do not feel an improved mood with your exercise, try increasing the intensity of your exercise. Another variation of this recommendation is to do a more intense seven minutes of exercise daily. The proponents of this approach suggest that a short exercise regimen will be easier to implement and sustain and, in the long run, the consistency will deliver the intended results of a healthier brain and body.

Spend time with people you enjoy. In an article published by the Times Magazine, social isolation was said to have the same impact on our health as smoking fifteen cigarettes a day. The study says that having a robust social circle lowers stress and improves mood. In life, there are people that you naturally feel comfortable with. Take time each week as part of your mental health regimen to seek out and spend time with people you enjoy.

Journal. Writing down your thoughts and feelings helps the brain processing of memories and can help you get a handle on your thoughts. The act of writing forces both sides of the brain to work together and can slow down the brain enough for one to get more coherent. The right side of the brain is the creative side that formulates ideas into a story and the left side is responsible for structure and prioritization. A good balance of both sides of the brain brings about more successful thought processing. Many people I suggest journaling to resist this practice because they fear that their private thoughts will be read by others. "What if someone else finds it and reads it?" I struggled with that thought at some point but decided I could not live my life in fear of others. Solutions could include journaling digitally and password protecting the documents. Or finding a lockable drawer and burning the journals at some point. You can also journal in pictures, scribbles, poetry or by formulating your thoughts and feelings into prayers. Whatever you do, find a way to express your inner emotions. Find creative ways around the fear. Do not let fear deprive you of a healthy practice. A very positive side effect of journaling is that you get pretty good at writing!

7

Working on the Mind

The first part of my journey in therapy majorly focused on brain health and lifestyle changes. The second and most extensive part focused on the mind. The brain and nervous system are visible organs and part of the physical body; the mind is an invisible place where our thoughts and beliefs are held. The state of our physical body impacts our health and relationships. However, in trying to recover mental health, it is not enough to work on one's physical health. So it was that I embraced the next level: working on the mind. I find Sigmund Freud's theory of the three levels of mind a good starting place to introduce the workings of the mind. Freud asserts that the mind is made up of three parts.

Freud's three levels of mind

1. The conscious mind
2. The subconscious mind
3. The unconscious mind

The conscious mind is the mind we are most aware of, where logic and critical thinking happen and the part of us that makes decisions. This is the part of the mind that decides that for better health, we will start going to the gym daily on the 1st of January. The conscious mind is powerful in choosing a direction.

Then there is the subconscious mind where we hold beliefs, feelings, urges, addictions, habits, automatic behaviours, irrational wishes, unacceptable desires, traumatic memories, creativity and intuition, slightly out of our awareness but accessible by introspection. The subconscious mind is thought to control the lion's share of behaviour. Using our earlier analogy, the conscious mind decides to go to the gym and the subconscious mind might have the idea that exercising is painful. With time, if the subconscious mind is not in alignment with the conscious mind, it might overpower the conscious mind and make us quit our exercising routine by 30th March. Most behaviour we fail to control is managed by the subconscious mind.

Besides these two minds is the unconscious mind which is outside our awareness and cannot be easily accessed but may show up in slips of the tongue and dreams.

The subconscious mind operates by "default programming". So, if the "programme" is not overwritten, it just keeps running the old installed programmes. Remember how I said it is not about you? Well, a lot of our behaviour is part of a programme and not consciously thought through. It takes reprogramming to change the automatic behaviours we do not like in our relationships. A lot of behavioural interventions focus on the conscious mind and end up falling far short of effectiveness. Advice falls in the realm of the conscious mind yet the real culprit of most of our negative behaviour is the subconscious mind.

Very early in my therapy, I was diagnosed with generalized anxiety. I was experiencing anxiety pretty much five days a week. The goal of anxiety treatment is to reduce or eliminate anxiety. The calming down of the brain is called soothing. When we are little and in distress, we are dependent on others to soothe us. Our primary caregivers may rock and hold us so that we are comforted and quietened. However, when we become adults, we are expected to have developed the skills to soothe ourselves. Suffering anxiety so frequently meant that my self-soothing skills were inadequate. So, self-soothing was a good early intervention for me in therapy. My therapist then quickly taught me a range of techniques that were meant to soothe the subconscious mind.

For most healing work, we have to slow down the conscious mind to help us become more aware of the subconscious mind's activity. The more aware we are of our mind's workings, the easier it is to manage and direct them. The conscious mind can be slowed down in the type of conversations that therapists hold with their clients. These conversations gently guide the conscious mind to healthier spaces and through reflective conversations, we begin to access the subconscious mind.

Since I discovered that most behaviour is controlled by subconscious programming. I started to research how to reprogramme the subconscious mind. I noticed that the most radical transformations to my mental and emotional state came not from reasoning ideas but from more indirect methods of work. The subconscious operates more in pictures and feelings than in words.

Step 1: Becoming Calm and Self soothing techniques

Breath work and controlling attention

The first technique is really simple. It is a matter of shutting one's eyes and focusing on one's breathing. In breath work, I was encouraged to breathe deeply, noticing each in-breath and each out-breath for as few as three to five minutes at a time. During this breath work, I was told that my mind would wander, and indeed it did. "What am I having for lunch? Is that assignment due tomorrow?" and so on, totally forgetting the breath. The instruction was to notice that my mind had wandered and to simply bring it back to the breathing pattern. This act of bringing the mind back to the breath was said to be critical to learning to control my attention. Attentional control is a key skill in building robust mental health.

Values-based meditation

The most effective of the techniques my therapist taught me was meditation. There are several meditation techniques. The one she taught me, focused on using one's values for meditation. She gave me about 100 little cards with various values printed on them. I sorted these values till I had only ten that were most important to me. She then asked me to go home and find statements that supported these values. These statements were famous sayings or quotes. On my return, we discussed one of my values and she taught me how to pace my breathing while repeating the phrase I had picked for this particular value. I was supposed to use the same "formula" on the other values and meditate two to three times a day.

It turns out that I never really got to the other values, but I did latch onto the first one and I used a combination of visualization of the verse as well as breath work. The value I chose first was 'solitude' and the saying I picked was "Jesus went up to the mountain and he prayed." The image I used was of Jesus walking up to the mountain at dawn and kneeling to pray. I learnt how to chant the phrase while breathing and visualizing. Within about two weeks of doing this, with about 50% regularity, I felt a dramatic shift in my sense of calm. I realized I was waking up calm and not anxious on most days. I was startled at how a simple practise could have such a huge impact.

Earlier, I mentioned that there is a part of our nervous system that is meant to keep us safe. It tracks every bad thing that happens to us and then keeps us scanning the environment for similar dangers in the future. Well, this system is called the 'sympathetic nervous system'. The job of this system is to keep us safe. It detects early signs of danger and prepares our bodies to respond appropriately in order to survive.

Everyone has this system. It is like an alarm that is activated automatically without our control. The alarm sends signals to the body to create stress hormones that prepare our muscles to be ready to fight, take flight or freeze. The stress hormones make our pulse rate go high and our breathing fast and shallow, our pupils dilate and energy is sent to our limbs. The entire system is primed for action. The system is good and is probably responsible for us humans surviving so well on this planet. However, every once in a while, it goes haywire and is over-activated. A broken sympathetic nervous system will cause stress hormones to linger in the body for longer than is healthy so that one feels a constantly high degree of stress. In such cases, people will begin to experience pathological levels of anxiety and depression.

To counter this emergency response system, we have another system called the 'parasympathetic nervous system' that is supposed to assess that the danger has passed and now work to bring us back to a state of calm. When we are in a state of panic, our energy-efficient system does not waste energy on growing and repairing our bodies at the time but saves up energy for action. As such, it is important that when the danger has passed, we return to a state of rest so that other important bodily functions like rest, repair and growth can happen. Another simplified name for the parasympathetic nervous system is the rest and digest system. This system can be strengthened by practising self-soothing. People who have a strong parasympathetic nervous system tend to be calmer and are found to also have deep slow breathing. The parasympathetic nervous system is responsible for the conservation of energy, transporting chemicals to cells, digestion, growth and repair. When the switch of the parasympathetic nervous system is broken, it is possible to switch this system on manually through controlled breathing exercises. That is why many guided meditations start out with an invitation to breathe deeply. We reach a calm state faster by just taking long, slow breaths.

Getting myself to a state of calm became a job. Breathing and meditation were working, although sometimes I was too agitated to meditate and just needed to go for a vigorous walk or run, or do jumping jacks on the spot. I have learnt to use a combination of strategies for different situations. Self-soothing is a technique I now treasure. It is common knowledge that the more we practice a skill, the easier it is to perform. So, just like any other skill, as I practice it over and over again, I become better at it.

In times of couple conflict, one of the reasons our struggles become intractable is because we fail to maintain a state of calm emotionally. Our conflicts often trigger our sympathetic nervous system so that we are agitated. The most common negative emotion in relationships is anxiety. However, other negative emotions rise up within us, like anger, blame, helplessness and overwhelm.

Nearly everyone can benefit from self-soothing skills. We all need to learn to quickly return the mind to a state of calm.

Soaking prayer

Looking back, I realize that I had learnt a practice that was perfect for calming me down in my Christian disciplines. I had picked it up some years earlier, at a Christian conference at Mto Moyoni in Jinja. The conference was "The Father Heart of God." The three-day teaching, in a nutshell, was to show Christians that God is not only a holy judge but a loving father too. God is not an impersonal force but a divine person, a father who wants to have an intimate relationship with us his daughters and sons. It was not very hard for me to psychologically grasp the idea. Whereas my father had died when I was three years old, I have been told stories of his gentleness and kindness. I also have a picture of him holding me as a baby and smiling lovingly at me. That picture as well as the stories corroborate the story of his reputation as an attentive, gentle father. This was merely an earthly father who had many faults as a human, yet managed to love well. At this conference, I understood at a much deeper level, that God's love for me was like my father's; not distant as I had once believed, but involved and engaged and a million times stronger than my earthly father's love. I also was reminded that I was a cherished daughter of the father.

I was also taught to activate that feeling of safety that I had as a child with my father in a method they called soaking prayer. I was taught to come to God not to ask for anything, but to just hang out in His presence as a cherished child in mutual love with a parent. For me, soaking prayer usually meant putting on some quiet music and lying on my back or curling up in a foetal position and creating a picture in my mind of me enjoying the father's embrace. I started to treat myself to daily morning soaking prayer. Often, I would drift off to sleep and I was told at Mto Moyoni that that was completely acceptable! I would wake up comforted and ready to face the world. I was reluctant to leave soaking prayer each time the time was up. It felt like drudgery to get back to regular life where my anxiety resided. Now that I understood the science of calming the brain, I could choose different methods to practice.

Mindfulness

I know I said that meditation was the most effective self-soothing technique but I think mindfulness comes very close. To me, mindfulness is paying attention to the present moment. It is using one's five senses of seeing, hearing, smelling, touching and tasting to tune in to one's environment. I mentioned earlier that the subconscious mind runs most of our lives. So many of our actions are so practised that we are not aware we are doing what we are doing. Once I get into my car on a workday, I do not have to give driving a second thought in order to get to work; it has become second nature. However, in living mindfully I try and practice these daily actions more intentionally. From the moment of my awakening, I try and use my senses to tune in to both my inward and outward environment. Tuning in to the body the moment I awaken and taking note of my feelings and sensations and taking the time to attend to those. Then on getting out of bed, mindfulness is becoming aware of the sensation of my feet touching the ground, noticing the weight and temperature of drops of water as they hit my body in the morning shower. Tasting each mouthful at breakfast, its quality and texture as I eat it, even breathing mindfully. Noticing the colours and shapes around me and stopping to notice the sounds in the environment. The most effective mindful practice for me is tuning in to how I feel on the inside of my body, observing both my emotions and physical sensations. This ends up making me sit very still as my attention turns inwards. Somehow, this leads me to experience peace. I am reminded of the Bible verse that says "Be Still and Know that I am God." It is as if God can only be known by the experience of stillness.

Other spiritual disciplines that lend themselves to self-soothing for me are: practising solitude, sitting in nature, worship, humming, reading sacred texts or philosophy and listening to sermons. All these can be helpful to calm the mind.

Safe place technique

Later on in counselling, I found a technique similar to what I had found in my spiritual retreat. My counsellor told me to think of a place that made me feel calm. I told her it was a little forest that was near the student accommodation at my university. It was a place I wandered to by myself and enjoyed when I wanted to be alone. She asked me to imagine myself there and to describe how I felt. I shut my eyes and told her that I felt a calm rising up in me as I imagined myself back in the forest surrounded by very tall trees. I could also see in my mind the sunlight piercing through the leaves. I described the smell of pine trees that filled my nostrils. My little forest also had a few butterflies and dragonflies flitting around, and the sound of birds. Deeper into the forest is a small man-made lake whose undisturbed surface is calm and its "sight" brings me a feeling of tranquillity. As I described this scene and spent time mentally wandering in my forest, I fell into a deeper sense of calm, my breathing slowed down to a steady pace, and I felt a warmth spread through my chest, all my troubles momentarily forgotten.

This, she told me, was a tool I could use at any point in time that I felt agitated and needed to soothe myself.

I have recently found that I can fall into deeper and deeper levels of calm. I am less reactive and my marriage is all the better for it. I can hold my tongue when I need to or let something pass where previously I used to feel that I would explode if I kept silent. I have learnt to calm myself down. In psychological terms, I have gained a higher level of emotional regulation.

From watching couples in therapy, I have learnt that it is almost impossible to teach anyone relationship skills when they are frightened or upset. The scientific explanation is that during these heightened states, the part of the brain that manages thinking and learning is hijacked by the one that is responsible for survival: the sympathetic nervous system again. One has to calm down before one can optimally access the parts of the brain that support learning. When a couple is mostly out of control emotionally, it is a good idea to get them to better levels of calm before teaching them skills. An important step in relationship counselling is supporting the couple to calm their emotions.

So, at that stage, I was calmer but not yet happy. Happiness was another thing altogether. But calm was an important precursor. Notice yourself when you get calmer. That is an important step to relationship recovery. The more I practice being calm, the more peaceful I am as a marriage partner.

Step 2: Becoming happy

It was great that I was calmer now. I was not calm every minute of every day. I was just calmer for a greater percentage of the times when I used to be distressed. As for being happy, this is how I got happy.

Maintaining happiness as we progress through life is a topic that is related to your psycho-social development. In the same way that we have physical stages of development from babyhood to adulthood, there are psycho-social stages of development from babyhood to adulthood. It is easy to tell what stage of physical development a human being is at because the physical development is visible. The words toddlerhood or adolescence hold much meaning for most people. We know that newborn infants cannot speak words or walk and teenagers get pimples and show major changes in their bodies, but very little knowledge is shared in the general public about psychosocial development. Psychosocial development is the ability to process thoughts, manage emotions and relate to others.

Psychosocial development is a process that we all go through; and just like the physical development stages, it is thought to have distinct developmental stages. To summarize a theory on it, Erik Erikson, a psychologist, says that there are eight psycho-social developmental stages. Each stage of life has a certain psychological goal and it is important for us to fulfil that goal in order to be content/happy and to get to the next stage of life. If one does not complete the goal, then they have to come back to it when they find themselves in crisis. It is thought that our ability to maintain happiness over our lifespan has a lot to do with how successfully we go through the different developmental stages[3].

3 https://en.wikipedia.org/wiki/Erikson's_stages_of_psychosocial_development#Wisdom:_ego_integrity_vs._despair_(late_adulthood,_60_years_and_above)

Erickson's Psychological Developmental Stages

Approximate Age	Virtues	Psychosocial Crisis	Significant Relationship	Existential Events Question	Events
Infancy Under 2 years	Hope	Trust vs. Mistrust	Mother	Can I trust the world?	Feeding, abandonment
Toddlerhood 2–3 years	Will	Autonomy vs. Shame/Doubt	Parents	Is it okay to be me?	Toilet training, clothing themselves
Early childhood 3–6 years	Purpose	Initiative vs. Guilt	Family	Is it okay for me to do, move, and act?	Exploring, using tools or making art
Middle Childhood 7–12 years	Competence	Industry vs. Inferiority	Neighbours, School	Can I make it in the world of people and things?	School, sports
Adolescence 13–19 years	Fidelity	Identity vs. Role Confusion	Peers, Role Model	Who am I? Who can I be?	Social relationships
Early adulthood Love 20–39 years	Love	Intimacy vs. Isolation	Friends, Partners	Can I love?	Romantic relationships
Middle Adulthood 40–59 years	Care	Generativity vs. Stagnation	Household, Workmates	Can I make my life count?	Work, parenthood

Generally, each one of us has a blueprint for different stages of life. If we achieve it, we are happy, and if we do not, we are sad. Happiness is achieving the goals that make up your blueprint.

Between the ages of twenty and thirty-nine (please note that the age boundaries may vary for different people and cultures), the main psychological goal most of us have is to forge intimate bonds. These are not merely acquaintance-ships, but relationships that are deep and meaningful. For many of us, the relationship of choice is marriage. Erikson stated that when we fail at this task, we end up isolated and this is very painful. This crisis brings many marrieds and singles to therapy. This often becomes the main crisis in those years and may continue to be a crisis well beyond the fifties if unresolved.

The stage before adulthood is adolescence in which Erickson named the life goal as developing a strong sense of self.

According to this Eriksonian theory, when intimacy fails, we must revisit the previous stage and complete its developmental task in order to succeed at forming intimate relationships. As such, when one's marriage hits the rocks, couples generally have to go through a degree of revisiting the previous stage of 'developing a sense of self' before intimacy. We need to look inward and understand and accept ourselves. After we have achieved that, we have a better chance of forging intimate bonds with others. However, if we have not yet established a strong enough sense of self, we will falter at forging strong bonds of intimacy with others.

A positive way to look at my marital distress was that our conflict forced me to revisit my sense of self as an individual. Knowing who I was and liking who I was were important parts of building my happiness. People who like themselves and are confident in who they are will make better partners. This is just how it works! Happiness and liking one's self are interlinked.

In the great wisdom of my mother tongue, Luganda, the word for enjoyment is "okweyagala" which directly translates to 'liking oneself'. Liking yourself and enjoyment are deeply connected. When you like yourself, your partner's actions do not pose as much of a threat to you as when you do not like yourself. In other words, the crisis is averted. If, however, you do not like yourself and sense that your partner also does not like you, then this is a major psychological crisis that can cause a lot of pain. Much of our attitude to ourselves is held in the subconscious mind. If you just observe your thoughts and attitudes, you can tell if you like yourself or not.

In therapy, I was particularly helped to rediscover my sense of self by the value sorting activity I mentioned earlier. I had been given over 100 cards; each one had one value written on it. Identifying my top ten would have been an overwhelming task. However, I was told to sort the values into three categories: very important, important and not so important to me. After I had done this, I was told to only keep the top ten values from the very important category. The way I achieved this was by asking myself, if I had to pick out only one value, which one would it be? So, I picked that value, and then I asked if I was allowed a second one, which one would it be? I allowed myself to pick one other and continued this process until I got ten. It was a wonderful feeling to look at my top ten values. My top ten values at the time were: integrity, social justice, beauty, order, contribution, adventure, faithfulness, solitude, spirituality, and family.

Identifying and thinking of my values gave my heart a surge of joy. It was as if I was discovering myself again. I was reacquainting myself with myself. Next, I was given an exercise in which I explored barriers to living these values and how to overcome these barriers. After this, I was taught how to validate my own values by finding famous quotes from any source that supported these values and as mentioned before, I used them when meditating. What I did not know was that I was validating myself in the process and giving myself support. We all need encouragement from time to time. By the time I went into therapy, I was mostly dependent on external sources for all my encouragement. I did not have a clear intention and habit of encouraging myself. Self-validation is about approving yourself and accepting who you are as you are, your needs, values and limitations. I mostly looked to Moses for this affirmation and when it would not come, I felt greatly let down. Practising my values was only one way of self-validation.

There are many other ways of self-validation. In my classes, I was taught self-care. Learning to take care of myself meant learning again to listen to my body: to rest when I was tired, eat when I was hungry, be kind to myself at all times. In doing this, I was reaffirming that my needs were important and slowly was coming back into balance. I could take care of others without neglecting myself. I realized I was as good at blaming myself as I was at blaming Moses. I would kick myself for not doing better or making a wrong decision. However, I learnt to be kinder to myself and to tell myself it was okay to make the choice that I made, or even the mistake. I was no longer holding myself to this perfect standard as I learnt to support, validate and love myself.

Naturally, the more I thought about my values, the easier it became to honour them. One of my values is social justice: it matters a lot to me that life is fair. So, I have endeavoured to find outlets for this side of me by being involved in social causes. This makes me happy. There was a shift in my life that came with all this work. My days were structured around honouring my values.

A new sense of purpose surged within me and I gradually started to feel more connected and engaged with life. I became happier.

Step 3: Reconnecting with others and spontaneous gratitude

Our psyches are hugely impacted and 'formatted' by the relationships we keep. As part of my rebuilding of self, I also worked on relationships with other people outside my marriage. I looked around and decided that there were people I had a natural affinity for and I cultivated those relationships and, for a while, neglected relationships that were giving me grief (this worked for me, but it is entirely an individual decision). I made it a point to weekly either schedule time to speak on the phone or do an activity with people that I enjoyed. I joined various groups like church groups and advocacy groups. In my friendships, I made sure that we got to more and more levels of openness with one another. I fought isolation; I could take more risks with people now because my mind was not as distressed and doubtful of the world and people around me as before. I was calmer, more confident and more trustful.

Somewhere along the way of getting calm, I found that a common feeling that I woke up to was gratitude. Once I had become calm and convinced at a subconscious level that the world was not an awful frightening place anymore, but a place where I had realized a great improvement in my condition, my courage to hope increased. Previously, I did not feel grateful spontaneously. I had to work on it. Yet now I noticed I was waking up grateful. All the work that we were doing in therapy to reduce anxiety and increase my sense of security allowed me to see the world through fresh eyes and it was no longer a great effort to see beauty all around once the internal hindrances were removed. I was happy with this new development.

It was important for me to become happy as an individual before I could recover marital happiness. David Riddell taught me, "The marriage is only as good as the spiritual and emotional health of the two people in it." It is like the metaphor of the ingredients and the cake. The quality of ingredients you put in is going to impact the final product. With marriage, the spiritual and emotional stability of the individuals is going to impact the marital stability. The more content and secure the individuals in the marriage, the better the marriage. This is why it is possible to greatly improve most marriages by just one person working on themselves.

Erikson was right; having a strong sense of self was indeed an important precursor to forging an intimate bond. Being happier meant that I was less demanding of Moses and was, therefore, less critical of him. This improved his own experience in the relationship. However, there were still some feelings of hurt in me.

Step 4: Healing Trauma

For most of my life, I did not understand that I was carrying trauma. The sudden death of both of my parents had left a psychological wound in me. I had no concept of trauma growing up, but I knew that I did not feel completely right inside. I was often sad and sometimes felt empty and easily got overwhelmed. My emotions were very volatile. My therapist arranged for me to have exposure therapy. However, exposure therapy was only mildly effective in reducing my burden of trauma. I could tell I was changing because I became more tender-hearted and was not as detached as I had been. However, exposure therapy, in my experience, did not give me enough healing.

One day during my training, I got very upset by a problem one of my trauma clients brought in. My supervisor and I discussed this and she recommended that I see an EMDR trauma therapist. EMDR stands for Eye Movement Desensitization Reprocessing. EMDR, like many good inventions, was discovered accidentally by a lady called Francine Shapiro. It is an unorthodox method that uses either tapping of the body, or an eye movement technique, to desensitize the body of a traumatic incident. It does not just use words to desensitize the body to certain painful memories but uses the mentioned physical methods along with verbal cues and imagery. I suspect that this is why it was more effective for me. It uses the language of the subconscious mind. The combination of physical, emotional and mental imagery has been found to effectively enhance the brain's reprocessing of painful memories to better resolution, reducing physiological disturbances that would typically arise from the painful memory. What was more exciting was that this therapy is much faster: it takes a few weeks to months rather than years. In fact, within the first few reprocessing sessions, I felt a great emotional load lift from my heart. I was a less irritable person, I slept better at night, and felt more whole.

All this therapy helped me to feel more connected to myself but not necessarily more connected to Moses. My connection to Moses was restored almost accidentally as you will see in the next chapter.

8

Step 5: Softening of the Heart

A: Empathy

By the time I got into therapy, my empathy for Moses was at an all-time low. Empathy is the ability to understand another's feelings from their point of view, capturing their position. I was not able to feel empathy for him. I tried to fabricate empathy but the kind I got was mostly superficial and intellectual. I could not feel his pain. This meant that I acted all the more unlovingly. For example, he would come home and report that his feet were burning. I would think, "Why do you choose to work so long and hard? You are simply reaping what you sowed!" Whereas there was truth in that, it was not the most loving response. We all do stupid things and then complain about the results, but when we turn to our loved ones, we need comfort at that time. I was unable to manufacture that comfort.

Empathy is not just an intellectual understanding but also allowing one's emotions to be touched by another's situation. A willingness to forget one's position for a moment and allow yourself to be affected by how the other person feels. It is seeing how the other person's position makes sense. It may require abandoning one's own position momentarily to put one's self in another's shoes.

To put it simply, what I was suffering from was a hardened heart. In my honeymoon years, I had a tender heart towards Moses. This tender heart made any work for him so easy. A hardened heart made work for Moses really a burden. Regaining a sense of empathy and tenderness was work that I needed to do. I am glad to have stumbled on the work of empathy in my class work. I say stumbled, but nothing of my journey was a stumble. I know that I was being divinely led through everything that happened on this journey.

Luckily, no one asked me to try to manufacture empathy through force of will as many methods do. Whereas those methods may work for some, they generally do not work for me. This is the story of how I regained empathy.

As part of my studies, I was given a task to draw a genogram of both my family and my husband's family. A genogram is a family tree. However, in addition to the usual information that family trees collect like name, age and physical ailments, in a genogram, there is more information that is collected. One of the unique pieces of information that are not found on ordinary family trees is the description of relationships in the family. In drawing a genogram, one has to trace what kind of relationships the principal person had with the different members of their family, but also relationships between other family members. There are different types of relationship bonds: harmonious, close, enmeshed (overly close), conflictual, abusive, distant or cut off and more. Combinations of these relationships can also be depicted. The class was not intended to teach empathy but rather to teach family systems. Yet for me, empathy was the by-product of the class.

The big assignment of this class was to trace three generations of Moses' and my family, starting with our grandparents. In order to recast such a tree, one is forced to seek out relatives. In my case, I reached out to three people: my mother's younger sister, my adoptive mum, and a cousin on my father's side. I was to list every person on the family tree, who they were married to, their dates of birth, marriage and/or death. I had to take note of mental and physical ailments, religion, occupation, levels of education and even immigration status.

An example of a Genogram[4]:

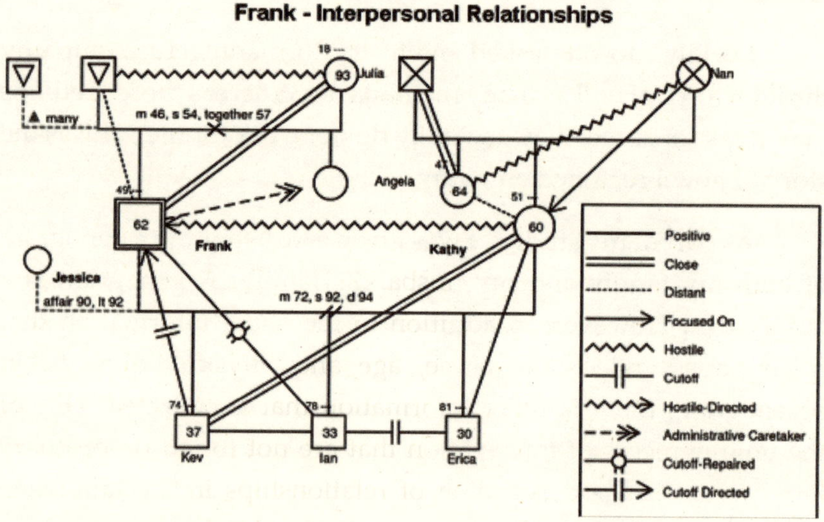

There were surprises in store for me in this work. Even though I already knew more than half of the people on the tree, new information kept emerging. On my mother's side, I discovered an educated great aunt who refused to marry, a rarity in her day! I was generally known as a non-conformist and was glad to learn

4 https://www.genogramanalytics.com/examples_genograms.html

that there were other nonconformists in my family, just like me! Then there was the fact that my grandfather was a catechist but my mum and some uncles shunned Christianity. I noted that my call to teaching was something that I shared with my grandfather.

Every time I work on a genogram with a client, something new comes to light and usually a greater sense of validation, belonging and understanding is fostered.

I learnt that my mother may have also suffered from anxiety. I started to see myself not as isolated, but as connected and part of a bigger family system. In drawing my genogram, I was once again validating who I was and psychologically bolstering my sense of belonging.

When I got to Moses' side, I was lucky because he had already drawn his family tree and I only had to find dates, medical and mental ailments, then begin tracing family bonds.

Tracing relationships on both sides of the family tree is very important since it is usually in the middle of relationships that our psyches are formed. For relationships, I asked Moses questions like: Who were you closest to growing up? Who did you not get along with? Who are you not in touch with now? What happened? I also spoke to one of his brothers, a storyteller, who gave me more nuanced descriptions of family relationships.

I captured major events like deaths, births, marriages and divorces. Putting the story into pictorial form really brought it to life. In the genogram, each female is represented by a circle and each male, a square. It was startling to see the number of squares and circles surrounding Moses – sixteen in total! I had never really understood the size of his family but seeing that row of seventeen shapes somehow gave me a new understanding. To indicate that a person died, we draw a big *X* through the circle or square. For me, that was very experiential.

After drawing a square for Moses and a circle or square for sixteen other siblings in a row, next was *exing* out his father's square to indicate his death on the family tree. This action sent a shock wave through me. I imagined the shock the whole family must have experienced when Moses' father died unexpectedly after a short illness. There were so many people Moses' father had been responsible for, so many that were affected by his death. I started to appreciate what his father's death meant to Moses.

As heir to his father, a huge responsibility was shifted in that event onto Moses' shoulders as an eighteen-year-old university boy. In the middle of his shock and bereavement, Moses became responsible for a small tribe. For the first time, I was able to appreciate how devastating that must have been. At that moment, I did not only know the devastation and anxiety it created for Moses intellectually; I experienced it emotionally. I started to understand the pressure that Moses lives under. I saw him in a different light. It was like seeing his broken, wounded heart and the frightening responsibility he carried! Something shifted in my heart.

This process helped me to understand Moses' drive and the long working hours. I finally understood why he had to work as hard as he did, and why he was so torn between being at home with me and our son or his work. I instinctively understood the impact that experience had on him then and its lingering impact today. I understood that he still carried vestiges of that shock internally! He had been thrown this really hard challenge when he was barely an adult. Suddenly, he had more than a grown man's responsibilities. His great sense of responsibility was now clear to me.

In a few short years after his father's death, his two younger sisters also passed away. I also had to *ex* out their two circles on the genogram. I saw that Moses, already sorrowful and overwhelmed with responsibility, had to take more pain. It was more than any young adult could cope with. This process impacted me so much and it softened my outlook.

When I looked at Moses, the story I told myself changed, he was no longer the man who abandoned me in the evenings. He was the eighteen-year-old who had suddenly found himself responsible for a large family. He was racing against time to keep up with their needs and he was doing the best he could. I could not separate the man I married from the painful past he carried as a child. This was a major paradigm shift.

Sometimes problems in marriage are created by wrong interpretations of others' behaviours and the stories we tell ourselves. In my case, I definitely was misinterpreting Moses' behaviour. The process of retracing our family setups helped me improve my understanding of the unique psychologies that make up our marriage. This helped me to have a more accurate interpretation of why Moses does the things he does. Our conflicts reduced greatly after that, not because Moses changed, but because my perspective changed.

I became less forceful when arguing about his taking time off work. Something in me softened. I have since used this process in therapy with clients, for them to see the person they are in conflict with in the context of the wider family and events of their lives.

Building empathy brings about a softening of one's approach to their partner. There are other ways to build empathy, but this was the way I was guided to. Now that I had grown some empathy, I was ready to work on forgiveness.

B: Forgiveness

By this stage, I had achieved a great amount of psychological stability. I was more confident in who I was and what I wanted out of life. I was honouring my values. I was both calm and happy within the community I had created for myself. I had more empathy for Moses and had a better understanding of our attachment insecurities. Yet feelings of resentment and bitterness that I experienced when I thought of past hurts kept coming in the way of further progress. I had willed myself to let go but I just seemed to never be done with the pain. I had tried several times to process my pain in pastoral counselling but in vain. I was stuck.

As God would have it, during the time that I was at Regent University, the chapel invited various speakers over a series of months to speak on the topic of forgiveness. These were world-class speakers that flew in from different corners of the US. I felt privileged to hear them speak. I felt that God was really helping me out. One speaker recommended praying for your offender diligently every day. He had set aside an hour to take a walk and pray for people that offended him. I did not feel up to this method at all. Somehow it just did not appeal to me.

Another talked about letting go and asking God for compensation. He wanted God to give him something better than what he had lost. It sounded like a bit of a trade. "Okay God, I forgive as you tell me to, and then you restore me to what I had before and beyond." I am not making light of this prayer. I often think along those lines when something bad happens. That was an option. I listened to all the different speakers and their methods but did not find something that worked for me.

At about that time, two parental figures recommended the book *Total Forgiveness*, a book much respected for its compelling biblical arguments in favour of forgiveness. The author, R. T. Kendall, pastored Westminster Chapel for twenty-five years. I read *Total Forgiveness* but I had to be honest with myself; it did not move the needle much for me in forgiveness. I did not agree with R. T Kendall. I was not able to give forgiveness by force of will and by reasoning. I knew that the Bible said to forgive, I also knew that if I did not forgive, the Bible said I would not be forgiven, but I needed something more to happen. I was honestly stuck.

During my second year of study at Regent University, I was honoured to join a marital research project called 'Hope Couples Project' led Dr. Jennifer Ripley an expert that worked with Dr. Ev Worthington to develop the Hope Focused Approach to Marriage. The people on the team were PhD psychology students and I was so lucky to be the only masters counselling student admitted to the project. For this, I will forever be grateful to Dr. Ripley. As part of our training on this project, we had to participate in clinical couple work, read two sizeable books cover to cover, watch a bunch of videos, and sit an exam. In this milieu of work, was a set of videos on Forgiveness by Dr. Worthington. By now, I was very interested in anything on forgiveness. Dr. Worthington had spent more than two decades studying forgiveness. He spoke so simply in the videos and explained forgiveness in a way that I could understand. It was logical, yet something about his simple words was really moving my heart. Within minutes, I felt that I had found something valuable.

The core of Dr. Worthington's transformative message was this: "When an offence is made, the difference between our expectations," and he held up one hand with palm facing down, "and our reality," he held the other hand in front of him with palm facing up, "creates an injustice gap." His gestures helped me see the gap between his hands. "Forgiveness is usually bridging this injustice gap," he continued. He had my undivided attention.

"Big gaps take more work and small gaps (narrowing the distance between his two palms) take less work. Forgiving is much helped by the humble attitude taken by the offending partner," he continued.

And when he added, "There are other alternatives to forgiveness," that tickled me and I could not wait for the list. "For example, there is revenge...." I could have hooted with laughter at the thought, an opportunity for mischief... but then he added another alternative to forgiveness: "...tolerance." *Really?* I thought, unbelievingly, and before I could finish my thought, his voice came through: "Not everyone will forgive...." I was really connecting with Dr. Worthington's view of forgiveness.

I liked knowing that I had options. He also encouraged that we should not rush into forgiveness. His words made sense. The way I was going about forgiveness in the past was with desperation to do it quickly, without fully appreciating what I had lost, or grieving it. It was as if I secretly feared that if I did not forgive quickly, I would never do it.

There were other things to work on. From a different angle, I realized that I had a lot of anger and frustration that I had stored up in my body towards Moses. One therapy session I attended taught me that emotions can be stored up as energy in different parts of the body, sometimes causing tension, knots and even pain. Once again, it was apparent that I needed to work on my subconscious mind to rid myself of anger.

One needs to rid the body of this energy. Violent exercises like kickboxing and jogging are good for this.

Back to Dr. Worthington's approach: his research had shown that the more time one spent in forgiveness work, the more forgiveness they achieved. "People who put in twice the amount of time in forgiveness achieved twice the amount of forgiveness." (I do not think we can measure amounts of forgiveness but you get what he means, right?) I was already putting in a lot of work. I now purposed that I was not going to be outworked. If extra work meant extra forgiveness, I was going to be doing extra work.

Dr. Worthington then laid out a five-step model to forgiveness called the REACH forgiveness model, where each letter stood for a step in the forgiveness process.

R = Recall the hurt.

E = Empathize with your partner.

A = Altruistic gift: Give forgiveness as an altruistic gift.

C = Commit to forgive.

H = Hold onto forgiveness.

His model was not based on willpower but rather on empathy. He had devised a way to help people get emotional forgiveness first before reaching decisional forgiveness. Getting the heart to move before the head worked for me.

I was able to use his method by following the videos without any other person guiding me and felt a great burden of past marital hurts finally roll off my chest. Dr. Worthington's REACH forgiveness model was so easy to use. Listening to him patiently and gently explaining what forgiveness is about really brought the model to life.[5]

I have used this model to help my clients when they struggle to forgive. Often, I will start them on building empathy by asking them to conduct some research around their offender's family context using the genogram tool I explained earlier. It is amazing what learning more about a person can do for you. It may not change events, but it can change your perception of them greatly!

One of my best examples of how empathy can transform a relationship is found in Stephen R. Covey's book *The 7 Habits of Highly Effective People*. In that book, he talks about being on the

---

5 To watch more of Dr. Ev Worthington's talk on forgiveness, go to https://www.youtube.com/watch?v=hXBMaOxloIs&list=PLUp8455lcz5kA1TWZPhxrRKfyN-V3D62LP

New York subway train on a quiet Sunday morning. The train was peaceful and people were enjoying reading the Sunday paper or just staring in silence when at one stop, a bunch of kids and one man got onto the train. The man sat down next to the author and seemed lost in thought. Meanwhile, the kids were noisy, jostling each other and disturbing the peace. Covey waited patiently for the man, whom he assumed was their father, to stop his children from this behaviour, but the father of the children did nothing. After a while, trying to hide his irritation, he asked the man if he would tell his children to not disturb the peace. The man seemed as if he had been roused from deep thought. "I guess I should," he responded wearily. "You see, we are coming from the hospital where their mother died an hour ago. I do not know what to think and I guess they do not know how to handle it either." Covey's irritation melted away instantly and was replaced instead with sympathy. He no longer wanted to stop the children. He wanted to help this man who had just lost his wife. This just goes to show that the back story really helps in the interpretation of a spouse's behaviour. This is what had happened for me in my family systems class. Giving an accurate context to one's actions can powerfully change our ability to tolerate or forgive their behaviour.

In counselling couples in the Drama stage, I often find that where there is low empathy, it is almost always a waste of time engaging forgiveness at the start. I have found it easier to guide the willing partner through forgiveness individually when their hearts have softened. First, there is building empathy, then I embark on using Dr. Worthington's REACH model.

For the 'R' stage (Recall the hurt), I will ask the client to write a letter that focuses on expressing their hurt to the other person. I ask them to hold off forgiveness at this point. This letter is about acknowledging loss first and acknowledging the damage. Even when I say that, most people seem in a great hurry to say they have forgiven. I think it works best if they sit for a while in their loss and acknowledge what they have lost. It is hard to forgive what you do not know you have lost. I assure them that they will not be sending this letter anywhere and that they can be candid about their feelings. When this letter is ready, typically in the second or third session of asking the client to write it, I use the 'empty chair technique' where I get the person to read the letter to the empty chair where they imagine their offender is seated. Most clients break down as they read the letter. At that moment, they let out to the other person what they have held inside for long, that pent up energy comes out of them. After the client has finished, I will usually sit in silence for a moment with them to honour their deep feeling and to empathize with them. This allows them to rest and grieve some. Then in a gentle voice, I tell them when they are ready to sit in the place of the offender and move to stage 'E' (give back an empathic response that the offender might have offered them). I may debrief with them before the exchange of seats on how they felt while reading the letter if I feel it is necessary.

In some cases, I encourage the person to come with a friend that they are comfortable with. I coach this friend in being supportive at the start of the session. They may lay a hand on the back or pat the arm when the forgiver is feeling broken. A friend also acts as a witness and validates the process even more.

For some clients, sitting in the offender's seat is what really breaks the unforgiveness and brings healing. It is hard to imagine what the offender will say that is satisfactory, but often when one lets their heart guide them, this too becomes a very illuminating moment. Some people really get into character and see for the first time how their offender might have felt. After this, I ask them to return to their own seat. When they have settled, I ask them whether they want to now offer forgiveness. I try and make it clear that they do not have to. Some clients will take a break of several sessions before getting to stage 'A' (offering the altruistic gift of forgiveness). Different people need different amounts of time for different reasons, be it anger, hurt or just time to grieve before coming back to this forgiveness work. When the emotions finally die down, some clients are better able to come to this stage where they give forgiveness as an undeserved or altruistic gift.

When they do utter the forgiveness, we move to step 'C' of the model (commitment to forgive). I usually ask them to write down a statement that they have forgiven this person and even date this note. Lastly, I teach the client step 'H' (Hold onto forgiveness), meaning that each time the emotions rise up and any second thoughts to reopen the injustice surface, that they remind themselves of their commitment. This usually gives clients stability of decision.

Throughout these stages, we scale the amount of hurt the client is experiencing. Generally, clients report that the degree of hurt reduces at the first two stages, enabling them to then offer forgiveness.

Forgiveness is a critical part of marriage work. Intimacy does not thrive in an atmosphere of resentment, anger or bitterness.

One has to rid one's heart of these emotions first before seeking intimacy.

Dr. Worthington's forgiveness model worked for me and got my heart to a great place to now rekindle emotional intimacy.

9

Getting Specialized Help with Emotional Intimacy

Up until this point I have mostly dwelt on changes that I made as an individual. I have talked about becoming calm, getting to happy, rediscovering myself, living a life that honoured my values, becoming more authentic and so on. By this time, I had already started seeing changes in our marriage and in Moses. It perplexed me. We had not attended couples therapy and Moses had not been to any individual counselling sessions. Even though I had shared a lot of information with him, I could not account for the change I was seeing. The change was greater than any work we had done together. There are things I had been asking of Moses for decades that he had found really hard to do consistently yet here he was doing them so naturally. He was coming home and totally putting away his work, on many nights instead of switching on the TV he would pull up a chair and sit and to talk to me, he was open to recreational activities I suggested and seemed to enjoy them, and was altogether more engaged in conversation.

One evening, we had had an especially blissful day and I had to ask, "What changed? How do you know exactly what to do to meet my needs?"

He just shrugged.

That question has come up a few more times and it seems mysterious how his transformation is happening. Whatever it is, the results I was seeing in my marriage were so good that I risked asking Moses again to venture into couples therapy with me. He agreed this time, just like that! I was overjoyed and surprised that there was not a bigger struggle.

I wanted to make sure that we had all the help we could get and were positioned for success. So, we opted to go to Dr. Doug Weiss, the founder of Heart to Heart Counselling Centre in Colorado Springs, Colorado. He specializes in working with couples that struggle to build emotional intimacy in their marriages. I had come across his videos on YouTube and found that he had such accurate descriptions of our specific problem. No other therapist had grasped the problem in our marriage. I felt that he was the most articulate couples therapist I had come across. I loved the fact that he had intensive therapy sessions, as a long-term therapy (over six months to two years) would not be workable for us as non-residents in the US.

There were couples at the Heart to Heart Centre from all over the world. The treatment was so well organized and logically structured that I felt we were in the most competent hands on earth.

Dr. Weiss is a specialist in marital intimacy. Through his therapy, we learnt that we were stuck in repetitive ways of relating to each other. Moses' primary pattern was one of creating distance and mine was one of constantly pursuing Moses. The pattern was ineffective and we were both considered to be in 'recovery' from our relational pattern. In other words, Moses needed to become aware of and change his strategies to create distance and I was to become aware of and change the constant pursuance of Moses (at least the over-functioning part). We had couple sessions with Dr. Doug Weiss that were highly insightful.

In addition to couple sessions and individual sessions with Dr. Weiss, we attended homogeneous group gatherings that were akin to Alcoholics Anonymous meetings. Distancers had meetings with other distancers and pursuers also had their own meetings. In these meetings, we admitted the repetitiveness of our behaviours and started to commit to ending our cycles. These groups were a great holding space for us. Physically sitting with other people dogged by similar pain was a great comfort. The programme also had very advanced language to describe the dance that had become our life and this was comforting. I felt extremely validated in this therapy. I hoped in my heart to create a programme similar to this one when I returned to my country.

Our treatment started out with a long personality assessment with a psychologist. This assessment guided Dr. Weiss on our unique treatment. Many sessions gently chipped away at whatever barriers lay in our way to emotional intimacy. The interventions given were very practical. I cannot share all of them here. It was not so much the practical suggestions but the careful way that each strategy built our emotional bond back. It is easy to share what the practical suggestions are but they lack their power if they are not in the context of the whole treatment that is aimed at bonding the couple together again.

Some of the easier strategies to share that allowed us to move past some of the deadlocks were so simple I wondered how we had been unable to think of them. For example, we had a problem of not liking each other's choice of recreation. Moses' idea of a date is often to watch a video. For me, that did not count at all as bonding time. I would want to take a walk or sit in a beautiful space, preferably outdoors, and talk. Dr. Weiss' programme got us to simply take turns in planning dates. Each week, the person planning the date plans it to suit their taste and the other has to happily support whatever is planned. The solution was so simple, and it definitely helped us enjoy a lot more recreation together. Although the idea is simple it comes from the radical idea that power should be balanced in the marriage.

One of the great things Dr. Weiss taught us about intimacy was that intimacy was a skill. I sat there in his office considering this new thought. It meant that like other skills, it could be learnt, and he emphasized how like any other skill, we needed to practice, practice, practice.

There are five practices he taught us that build intimacy. He encouraged us to have fifteen minutes of exclusive time together daily, eyeball to eyeball, preferably when we were not too tired, and to share:

Two feelings a day

Two prayer requests

Two compliments

Making vulnerable invitations to our partner

Affirming our partner's beauty of soul (heart and mind) and body.

He gave us special formats for this work and we practised in his office while he coached us on how to complete these practices in a way that would give the most impact. We followed his plan religiously for thirty days. There were many other aspects to the therapy but these daily practices were magical for me. They met that inner need for my soul to feel connected to Moses' soul and I experienced great intimacy. I felt more emotionally connected to Moses than I had in a very long time. We also became more sexually attuned to each other.

After 30 days, we became more erratic about these practices. At first, I was really unhappy about this because I felt I had found our happily ever after magic pill and felt really frustrated that Moses was not willing to practice every day. However, my fights were taking us backwards. I realized that our marriage was so much better than it had been that I decided not to fight about doing our daily exercises. Although we did not do our daily exercises as they were prescribed, we decided to more naturally incorporate these practices into our lives. Our conversations changed in that we now knew the ingredients that were key in connecting more deeply. We were careful to incorporate clear descriptions of our feelings daily and had a stronger bond. I was fascinated by this therapy and how a five-day intensive therapy can make such a difference in a couple's life.

Thankfully for us, even when we seemed to not be fully engaging in our new exercises, another therapy was also impacting our marriage for good. I had learnt it theoretically in school and had felt its potential even on the first reading of the textbook. Most of the marriage and family therapists in my school department were using it. It was also attachment-based and focused on repairing the couple's emotional bond. This therapy is called Emotionally Focused Therapy (EFT) or sometimes Emotionally Focused Couple Therapy (EFCT). It was first developed and tested by Dr.

Sue Johnson and Dr. Les Greenberg in 1985. It is so recent that there are still so few EFT certified therapists worldwide.

These are some of the gleanings I picked from this therapy:

- Our attachment bonds, although invisible, have been studied, can be understood, fall in a few understandable patterns and can be modified to increase satisfaction.
- When we have strong emotional bonds, we feel safe and can face anything. When we are missing strong bonds with others, nothing seems right.
- Threatened emotional bonds have a strong impact on our general well-being.
- It is normal to be distressed when distanced from our loved one or to mourn if we lose the relationship.
- The fights that couples have are less about ideas and more about bonds. So, the therapy focuses less time on arguing ideas and more time on rebuilding the couple bond.
- Good emotional bonds are what we use to decode marital communication.
- Rebuilding a strong emotional bond often solves communication problems even without teaching a couple communication skills.
- Without emotional bonding, it is difficult for couples to effectively get through to each other.
- This approach is less about arguing and appealing to the conscious mind with logical arguments as most couple therapy used to be but focuses on helping the couple

access their deepest emotions and vulnerably share them with their partners.

- When couples fight and attack each other, they are really frightened on the inside. They are in need of love and reassurance but have been triggered to panic. Their system of communication has been hijacked.
- Pursuers' anger is often more about a fear of abandonment and distancers are usually feeling a fear of engulfment (This is to over simplify).
- Underlying most fights are the questions "Do you love me?" "Do I matter to you?" " Do you like me?" "Will you be there for me?" but these very intimate questions are covered up with much stronger and less vulnerable words and actions.
- Vulnerability is about opening one's heart and exposing one to the possibility of being hurt again. It feels risky and yet it is the way back to intimacy.

So EFT is about helping the couple hold these vulnerable conversations. Sue Johnson mentions research where twenty sessions were sufficient to restore the couple bond. However, this is not prescriptive. These vulnerable conversations are what repairs the couple bond. Most couples, after cycles of conflict, block off their hearts to each other so that they no longer express their primary vulnerable emotions to each other. Instead, what they share are secondary strong emotions. For example, when one feels betrayed, they may express anger but hide their grief. The relationship does not feel safe enough for one to show their grief. Whereas expressing grief would be more likely to elicit a loving response from the spouse, the grieving partner denies their grief and instead expresses anger. The anger they express will mask their more vulnerable feelings and send an inaccurate message to their spouse. Meanwhile, this anger is also likely to provoke a distancer to defensiveness or shutdown.

A really neat depiction of the strength of vulnerable emotions happens in the animated movie *Inside Out*. Five emotions are depicted as the main characters: joy, sadness, fear, anger and disgust. As the plot unfolds, we get to see how each emotion plays an important role in life. For a while, though, we do not see the role of sadness. It seems as if sadness has no role. Then eventually, towards the end, it happens so briefly that you could miss it, sadness' role is depicted. Sadness is shown as an emotion that has the power to draw out protection and support in others. Sadness is a very important emotion in our humanity. Think of funerals in Uganda where sadness is freely expressed. I am proud that we allow ourselves to wail and sob and verbalize our grief in long monologues. This expression touches the hearts of the mourners in such a way that they respond appropriately to the bereaved family. They gather around them, hold them, and sing to them in a way that they otherwise might not, had they not understood the mourners' sadness.

The aim of EFT therapy, therefore, is to get the couple to use the more vulnerable emotions to become more connected to each other and gently guide them back to a place of trust and cooperation where the couple can reach out to each other in times of need. Research shows that 90% of couples that go through EFCT report an improvement in their relationship and that these gains are sustained over varying periods of time

So it was that Moses and I started to use these strategies in our relationship. Exposing our fears rather than our stronger emotions. We learnt to slow down and feel the vulnerable emotion, stopping long enough to own it and then presenting it in a natural way to each other. By "natural" I mean in a way that the tone of voice, demeanour and words all convey the same message.

Beyond sharing vulnerable emotions, EFT takes the couples to another level. Once the relationship feels safe enough. EFT helps the couple express their needs by verbalizing their requests for comfort and support.

When couples attack each other, often what they are really saying is simply "my needs are not getting met". But rather than express, "I need you," most of us present, "You are so useless because you do not meet my needs!" As anyone can imagine, this kind of message is a recipe for disaster. Sometimes all I want is for Moses to "hold me tight." But I often cannot get myself to formulate this request in a congruent way. Similarly, he will struggle to express some more vulnerable requests for emotional support. So, learning to communicate our needs is also a work in progress.

I must say that the key change in EFT is said not to come from understanding, as it is from the couple allowing themselves to experience all the vulnerable emotions that they kept hidden away from each other. So, the therapist's job is to guide the couple in the expressing and feeling of underlying, denied emotions and amplifying them. Emotions are the key to the change that builds back the secure attachment bond.

Conclusion: A Few Beautiful Stories of Connection

Moses and I are now using potential conflict interactions to connect emotionally. For example, recently Moses invited people to our home without consulting me. I discovered this a couple of evenings before the event as he asked me to join him in hosting them. My first thought was that he had gone ahead to think about the idea, and had invited the guests without consulting me. I felt left out! Typically, this would result in me fuming over the thought that he was doing things on his own and my anger would spark a fight where I would attack the whole idea.

With my new skills, instead of attacking, my negative feeling caught my attention and piqued my curiosity. I paused to examine my offence and asked myself, "What is the more vulnerable feeling under the feeling of anger?" I discovered that I was feeling left out, excluded.

To paint a picture, just imagine being on a playground as a child and watching other children play while not being invited to join in. That is how I was feeling. Just vulnerable, uninvited and unwanted.

In the pause, he noticed that I had a struggle and when I spoke up, my tone of voice and my words expressed the hurt of feeling left out instead of an attack. I was congruent! Exactly as I was on the inside as on the outside. He got the message! He reached out, squeezed my hand and gently apologized. He then let me know that he had no intention of leaving me out. His expression of understanding was sufficient for me to feel he "got" my feelings and the issue really became a non-issue! We bonded at a critical point of insecurity.

In past years, there would have been anger and accusations and defences about how our family should go about invitations. The matter would most likely end up in a stalemate. We are now finding ourselves in a more intimate place after conflict. I am not coding my hurt and vulnerabilities in misleading stronger emotions. Anger was one of the main emotions I felt and used to attack in the relationship. It was various fears under the criticism and accusations. Now there is something more tender, more vulnerable. A part of me I had denied.

Another example was a time we were supposed to go to Saturday church. For whatever reason, Moses did not show up in time for church at the agreed time, so I went alone. The next day on Sunday, I was expecting to spend the whole day with him. It was our catch-up day. However, no sooner had we finished breakfast than he started to put on his shoes.

"Where are you going?" I asked.

"To church," he replied.

Once again, the feeling of abandonment started to rise and before it could turn into an angry attack, I paused and, lowering my head, tried to feel the vulnerable feeling inside. Once I had identified it (this only takes seconds), I said to him that I was going to feel lonely since we had committed to going to church the previous day and I had expected to spend the whole day with him. Once again, my voice and slightly lowered gaze matched my words. I was no longer giving mixed signals.

He stopped and looked at me and said in a husky voice, "Do you want me to stay?" His tone of voice helped me understand that he was attuned and there was an openness to this offer. I felt that he was truly willing to give up his plans for me. He too was congruent. His non-verbal language matched his words. I understood that if it was that important to me, he was happy to stay.

By now, I had owned my feeling of loneliness and told him that I would wash my hair while he was away. "How does washing your hair take away your loneliness?" he asked with incredulity. I was a little tickled by the mismatch of my statements and noted that he was really present. My heart was glad.

"It just gives me something to do," I told him, smiling at the disjointedness of my ideas.

"I can stay if you want," he offered again.

By this time, I was fully reconciled to the fact that I would cope. "No, you go. I will be okay." And I really meant it.

Before he left, he stood at the door and opened his arms to me. I approached him and he gave me a fierce hug. That one hug communicated, "I hear you, I care about you, and I love you!"

Our lives have changed. I have gone back to being able to feel my feelings and having the courage to share them as they occur. Moses picks up these feelings and is more attuned to me. Using Dr. Doug Weiss' method, Moses will now share more about how he is feeling even in random text messages during the day. Sharing our feelings honestly and being able to respond to each other in a more attuned way has been a major change.

The other principle that I have heard of that seems to have played out in our marriage is that you attract who you are. There are times I ask Moses how he came to change so much over the past years. I usually want to crack open his skull to find out what his own journey has been. He simply says that perhaps it is me who has changed. So, perhaps it is a case of you attracting who you are. The more vulnerable I am, the more I draw out Moses' vulnerability.

This book has taken me nearly three years to put together. I have tried to simplify a three-year course into the bones that make up marital intimacy for an ordinary person. At the time of my conclusion, I am quite happy with what I am able to offer the world through this writing. I hope those who are in intimate relationships and those who are not, will all be helped by these strategies.

I wish you greater intimacy in your relationship!

The end

Bonus Section: Practicing Emotional Stability and Other Relationship Principles

One of the key skills responsible for our stability is the ability to meet first, our own emotional needs, and then each other's needs. This skill is a keystone skill. My brain's default setting has changed to calmer and more settled where it used to be anxiety. I am now less likely to get irritable or angry. With meditation, I have even learnt to generate joy and wholeness from within. Getting rid of anxiety and anger has left me a whole lot more energy to deal with everyday life. I am learning to manage my internal world so that I can generate any emotion I want. Wouldn't it be wonderful to feel tender-hearted in the marriage whenever one wanted? I believe that like all other skills, this can be achieved with specific practice!

Like many couples, Moses and I have had communication problems where I felt we were sitting on a backlog of problems that never seemed to get solved. This is where a lot of therapies will attack listening and speaking. However, according to attachment science, poor communication in intimate relationships is not about listening and speaking but boils down to a lack of emotional attunement. This is the real problem the couple is facing. Emotional attunement is the ability to recognize, engage and understand another's emotional state. This is all part of a secure attachment system. In insecure attachment, we often will be in one form of anxiety or another. When we are feeling threatened and anxious, we tend to behave in selfish or self-preserving ways. Anger is one good tool for self-preservation. The body's resources during anger are focused to prepare for attack. It is not time to be creative with our expressions. On the other hand, if we are feeling safe, the mind and body's resources are not being used up in preparation for an attack and, therefore, we are better able to be more skilful at communicating. So, during conflict, communication distortions ensue out of our anger and anxiety. This is the real issue underlying most miscommunication in the Drama stage of marriage. That is why when the emotional bond of the couple is built back, most communication problems simply disappear.

It is possible to attain higher levels of communication even after the emotional bond has been restored. In our training, we were taught three layers of communication: Facts, Feelings and Values. When we are not attuned in marriage, we mostly share the first level of communication: facts. We speak about what we did and things that happened in our day.

For example, in the past, I would ask Moses about his day and typically I would receive a news bulletin. "I did this and that and the other and so and so did this…." etc. It was hard for me to stay interested in such conversations. I was hopelessly unaware of why I just could not pay attention. Emotional language, the medium through which we bond, was lacking in our conversations.

The other layers of conversation were lost to us. A person with high emotional attunement would be able to discern the deeper implications. I did not have the skill of reading and understanding his emotion or the deeper, more abiding values.

Let me expound on this with an example. Imagine after a long day at work, your spouse saying, "We moved office today at work." This is a fact.

You might respond with, "Oh, wonderful. Congratulations!" Or you may follow up with, "So, how do you feel about it?" Don't be surprised to hear a totally different story as told through feelings: "I feel disappointed because I got the cubicle next to the smelly toilet and Jim got the one I wanted next to the window. I don't even know how I will get my work done." Your spouse is disappointed, dejected and maybe even jealous of Jim and identifying the underlying feeling accurately helps you respond appropriately.

A good question to follow up the above revelation of feeling disappointed is, "What was the worst thing about getting the move for you?" How they answer will help you understand their heart. Conversations are more engaging when people communicate feelings and when those feelings are expressed in a convincing manner.

One of the uses of therapy is to help people become more proficient in identifying their feelings and in expressing them more congruently. This skill is then taken out of the counselling room and used in everyday life.

Moses and I had been practising how to speak on the feeling level for a while now. This has changed the dynamic of our relationship. We are able to tune in to each other better when we communicate. Beyond feelings are values. Values are standards that one considers important for their life. This is very critical information for spouses to get to know each other. In the above story, the spouse whose office had moved might have a value of beauty, relishing beautiful spaces at work and at home. Once you can understand someone's values, their behaviour starts to make a lot of sense. A person that values beautiful spaces might be unproductive and irritable when the house is messy. Thinking that perhaps they are unreasonable will just spark a fight. Acknowledging that this is just how they are wired can lead to supporting them to have a more orderly beautiful space. Understanding values like these with time helps you get to know your spouse's heart.

So, we are employing the skill of curiosity in getting to understand our values. Getting to really understand your partner's values helps you to build intimacy.

Once you know your spouse's values, then you can go about supporting them in honouring their values. When we live according to our values, we are truly happy. One of my values is social justice. So, if I am working on a community project, if Moses tried to hinder me or dissuade me from it, that would create conflict. Yet if Moses found ways of encouraging me to go for it and support me in my work, this would make me feel his companionship.

It takes much practice to be able to identify feelings accurately underneath the facts. For some people, this comes naturally. Yet for some of us, it takes a lot of practice. I have to work much harder at this skill than some people. You and your partner can acquire this critical skill for intimacy.

These skills are lifelong skills in that there is no end to growing them. I recall once my supervisor pointed out that there was a hint of triumph underneath my client's anger. This level of advanced understanding of emotion is what we are gunning for. This is going to be a lifelong study. No rush, take your time. As long as you keep making progress, you will get to a place where emotions are easier to decipher and this skill makes a difference in relationships.

Here is a note of caution: it is easy to focus on your spouse and how well they are developing the skill of deciphering feelings. This can create tension and even resistance to growing the skill. The better approach is to focus on yourself, on understanding and naming your own emotions. Commit to mastering these skills. Communicate your feelings and values when you speak. A simple way to become more emotionally self-aware is to journal your feelings and values. You can even journal about how you feel when your spouse does not share their feelings! So, this is a call for you to be what you want others to be. This is the best contribution you can make to your family! It is also my firm belief that if you consistently practice these skills, your family will become more like you.

Lastly, on communication, words in themselves are only 30% of communication. Getting your words to match your tone, body language and true feelings is really where the bulk of communication happens. This will be something to work on for a lifetime.

At the height of our drama, I used to show Moses anger when in truth I was lonely. I displayed criticism when I felt unloved. He would stonewall when he was hurt and create distance if he felt overwhelmed. However, we have started to be more skilled in reading each other and in communicating how we truly feel inside.

I will share a recent example. I was preparing to take on a sizeable order of Christmas baskets from one of my business clients. In the middle of the joy and excitement of the preparations, my client called to cancel his order. I was greatly disappointed. In the evening, I relayed the story to Moses. I do not think I was so congruent in expressing my disappointment and hurt but I did show my frustration. I suddenly noticed that Moses was quiet, looking down and had put his palm on his cheek. I stopped talking and we sat in silence for a while. I have learnt to stop and observe body language for clues.

I became curious about this new posture that he had adopted. Generally, I would say he looked sad, but I had no clue what he could be sad about. I was emotionally out of touch with my disappointment at that time. Then it dawned on me that in his silence, he was expressing disappointment. I checked in with him to see if I was reading him accurately and he affirmedmy observation. He was disappointed on my account! This melted my heart. I felt not only so completely understood but also felt comforted because he had accurately understood my situation and had an appropriate response. What I want you to note, though, was that it was his non-verbal cues that spoke for him. He did not say, "Oh, how sad!" or "I am feeling sad for you." Moses was not saying much verbally, but his actions were saying tons! One of my professors used to say, "Listen with every part of your body." As married couples, this is a helpful skill.

Although we had a major lack of skill in maintaining our emotional bond in our marriage and have had to do a lot of work in that area, some things were working for us, strengths that we had as a couple. I believe these have especially helped us to come to a good place. I will call them five precursors. These precursor strengths helped our journey to be easier and more fruitful.

Precursor 1: Integrity, honesty and reliability

It is said that the word integrity comes from the word integer which means one whole. When someone has integrity, they tend to be the same internally as they present externally. They are not phoney or pretentious. They are comfortable showing who they are to the world. Out of integrity comes honesty and transparency. Honesty is speaking the truth even when not asked. Transparency is being open to scrutiny and having nothing to hide. Moses and I have a good mix of honesty and transparency in our marriage. We speak the truth to each other and sometimes this can be a hard truth. I tend to be blunter and he gentler with the truth. At the end of the day, we both value honesty and integrity.

Honesty will cause you to openly confess things that your spouse ought to know about even when you feel ashamed of them. Intimacy does not thrive in a situation devoid of honesty. A lack of honesty breeds mistrust. Mistrust and intimacy are incompatible.

In Western Uganda where I was nurtured as a young Christian, honesty was top of the list as a sign of conversion to Christianity. Open confession of sins was the order of the day and people publicly returned items they had stolen. These were good examples that enabled us to practice the courage of speaking the truth and changing one's life to match one's own talk. Honesty takes courage, and courage is both an emotion and a skill that can be learnt.

Having integrity also means we are generally reliable people. I can depend on Moses' word and he can depend on mine. This is not to say that we are perfect. There are areas we need to work on; but on the whole, we cultivate a culture of reliability in our marriage. You might be a person of integrity who married someone who lacks integrity or vice versa. Wherever you are on this journey, start to grow your own integrity and reliability.

This is a stabilizing factor in marriage. It is a choice we all have to continue making every day in every situation.

Precursor 2: Knowledge of principles

Moses and I agree that there are laws that govern various systems. If you can understand the laws and systems, you can then manage outcomes. So, we are always learning together. We share the value of knowledge. This value has made us open to learning the principles that govern relationships. This has been a big plus because as our minds grasp knowledge, our practices change. Relationships, just like any other area in life, are governed by principles that you need to learn. The easiest parallel I can think to point you to is money. The principles of making money have been studied and can be passed on. If you learn the principles and apply them, you can accumulate it. If you do not learn the principles or do not apply them, however much is given to you, you will lose it. The principles of relationships have also been studied and, in this book, I hope you have picked up a number of them. So, whatever you do, gain knowledge of the principles that govern relationships. There is something important to note, though. Knowledge alone is not enough. Our deeper attitudes are a programme running that is not easily changed by just knowledge. Just like with money, knowledge alone is not enough. One has to have the right attitude and practices to be successful. This is the same with relationships. Knowledge is a start; attitudes and practices complete the cycle. Attitudes are usually set (psychologically programmed or installed) very early in life and hard to change, the attitudes to relationships are set very early in life and can be hard to change. If you find yourself stuck, unable to change your patterns, running in circles, again and again, you are likely dealing with subconscious mind programming. A professional therapist can help you get unstuck and deal with subconscious barriers in your mind.

Precursor 3: Take individual responsibility

David Riddell says, "The marriage is only as good as the spiritual and emotional health of the two people in it." This means that each individual can make an improvement in the marriage by just working on their own spiritual and emotional health. You can stop right here and determine what things you can do to improve your spiritual and emotional health and start to do them. You will reap a reward. Take personal responsibility.

In most marriages in turmoil, a lot of blame is going on. Each person is looking to the other to change. I was always one to blame. It took me a while to start to change and I still slip up regularly and that is okay. Blame is usually a recipe for disaster and a sure way to disappointment. I had to be told half a dozen times in therapy, "The only person you can change is you." You cannot hang your hat on someone else changing. In therapy, this is a very important step to get clients to focus on their own change, to see their own contribution to the marriage mess. It is great progress once one shifts to this position. It is an indication of real progress.

Precursor 4: Invest attention, time and money

As a couple, we invested a lot of attention, time and money in getting back on track. A day did not go by without me thinking of our problems and either processing my thoughts and feelings in a journal, reading something about marriage, or practising spirituality. We put in hours upon hours of work towards this.

Initially, I felt that I was doing this work alone. Eventually, Moses started to get interested and participate.

The principle of sowing and reaping also works in relationships. Do not invest nothing in the relationship and hope to reap a lot! These are basic principles of life. You reap what you sow. Put in more, get out more. Studies show that happily married couples spend more time together than unhappily married couples, on average about forty minutes daily together. Be intentional.

Plan to spend something in terms of attention, time and money/resources. Put aside time daily, weekly, monthly and annually. Daily time could be time to catch up with each other, or to serve each other, pray and eat. A weekly date protected from problems, distractions and interference helps much. Monthly, you might spend a weekend that is focused and, annually, a holiday. I also encourage you to read books; talk about these things with your friends; attend fellowships, workshops and conferences. As for money, I told you initially we were put off by what we considered a high fee for a five-day intensive therapy, but by the time we finished, we had spent much more than that. Investing in your marriage early will likely save you spending lots more later. Don't give up if there is a cost to getting better. Be ready and willing to make some sacrifices. Small incremental investments will pay off in the end.

Precursor 5: Environment

The environment in which you grow your marriage is important. Surround yourself with people that know more than yourself in this area. Again, this is a simple principle that works for almost any problem. If you want to learn something new, surround yourself with people who know more and have succeeded in that particular area than yourself. Observe them, and also ask them to teach you.

There are skills and ways of thinking that are necessary to grow emotionally and spiritually in marriage. One of these skills, for example, is emotional self-awareness. There are communities where emotional self-awareness is very low and spirituality is not valued. Your development is going to be negatively impacted in such communities.

In my School of Psychology and Counselling, we had to identify feelings and values embedded within people's conversations on a regular basis as part of our skills training and we were encouraged to make this a way of life. Our goal was to become more authentic, connected individuals. Many of my professors and classmates were much more emotionally articulate than I was. Being in a community like that was important to help me grow in my own self-awareness. I also immersed myself in a spiritual community and now I endeavour to spend time with friends who can speak in both emotional and spiritual depth. One of the benefits of therapy is being in close proximity to someone who knows more than you in relationships. Professionally trained therapists will know how to help you increase the depth of your awareness in communication in both areas.

Consider small ways that can move you away from detractors of progress towards catalysts of emotional and spiritual development.

Moses and I were more present and looked forward to our interactions. We focused on relaxing when we got together. We were intentional about activities that were rejuvenating. We enjoyed massages, good conversations, having friends to meals, touring new places. We also learnt to protect times when we minimized distractions. Moses has been quite consistent in taking me on a weekly date for more than a decade. So, we use those times and other mini snatches of time to really connect.

Parting Remarks

The greatest task in healing the insecure attachment is self-soothing. The common feeling underlying all insecure attachments is anxiety. Even though the anxiety plays out differently, it is all anxiety. The anxiously attached individuals will show more of a fear of abandonment, loneliness and feelings of worthlessness. Dismissively attached individuals will show a fear of intimacy and fear of loss of freedom. Fearful avoidants will show a fear of being hurt and at the same time a fear of abandonment. Each spouse needs to recognize their own brand of anxiety and heal it. Recognizing these feelings early and owning them rather than blaming your spouse for them is critical. Then, and only then, can you succeed in resolving them. What works for me when I am alone is just stopping and acknowledging how I feel. As I sit in that emotion, I then decide how I want to comfort myself. I may reach out to Moses or another friend, or I may lay in a foetal position with my arms around my neck and my knees pulled to my chest or sit with my arms around my neck in a self-hug. I also shut my eyes and do my deep breathing exercises. However, the most effective strategy for me is imagining myself in an embrace. Almost immediately, a stillness comes over me, warmth starts to spread from my heart throughout my chest and I feel special and loved. In time, it has become easier and easier for me to self soothe. My goal is to make this my prevailing internal state.

Being able to soothe myself has reduced the great burden from my avoidantly attached husband. My increasing emotional stability has given him more freedom to be loving. Whereas distance frightens an anxiously attached spouse, the feeling of being smothered and obliged frightens the avoidantly attached spouse. With this knowledge, I am able to know when to hang back a bit. By softening my pursuit for closeness, I made the relationship feel much safer for Moses. Once Moses realized that he was not going to be overwhelmed by my needs, he was able to eventually relax and be loving. The pursuer and distancer both make up a marital system that has a delicate balance. A delicate balance seems to be a factor in all natural systems. Once you understand that, you can accept it and work with it. We have become better at maintaining that balance. Each one of us creates more stability.

Finally, I would want to believe that everyone who loves hard enough will be rewarded by a reciprocation of love. Yet not even the God of the universe secures this from us but leaves us our free will to love him back or to reject him. More often than not, when we change, our partners find that the dynamics of the relationship have changed and they are forced to change too. Yet we have no control over our spouse's change. As a marriage therapist, I have had to accept that some marriages will survive and some will not. Yet, whether a marriage survives or not, the healing of the individuals is possible as long as they reach for it. What all of us need is to feel emotional security. We want to feel whole, loved and worthwhile. Each one of these emotions happens inside our skin and is within our control. Much deeper than the need to keep the marriage is the need to feel secure and lovable inside our own skin, and with what I have already shared, you can achieve this, whether your spouse co-operates or not. Once you take this pressure off the marriage, the marriage has a much better chance of success.

About the Author

Pendo Kisakye Galukande nee Zirimu has been married to the love of her life Prof. Moses Galukande for 24 years. They have an adult son. Pendo received her primary education at Kitante Primary School in Uganda's capital city- Kampala and her secondary school education at Maryhill High School in Western Uganda where she was a head girl. She attained a Bachelors in Zoology at Makerere University before attaining a Master of Science degree in Health Systems Management from University of London, London School of Hygiene and Tropical Medicine. She went on to Regent University in Virginia Beach, Virgina, USA where she completed a Masters in Couple Marriage and Family Counseling. She sees clients at Healing Talk Counselling Services, and runs a social enterprise that promotes employment and mentorship to youth through the manufacturing of hand crafted gift boxes and cards. You can read more about her social enterprise at www.disndat.co.ug